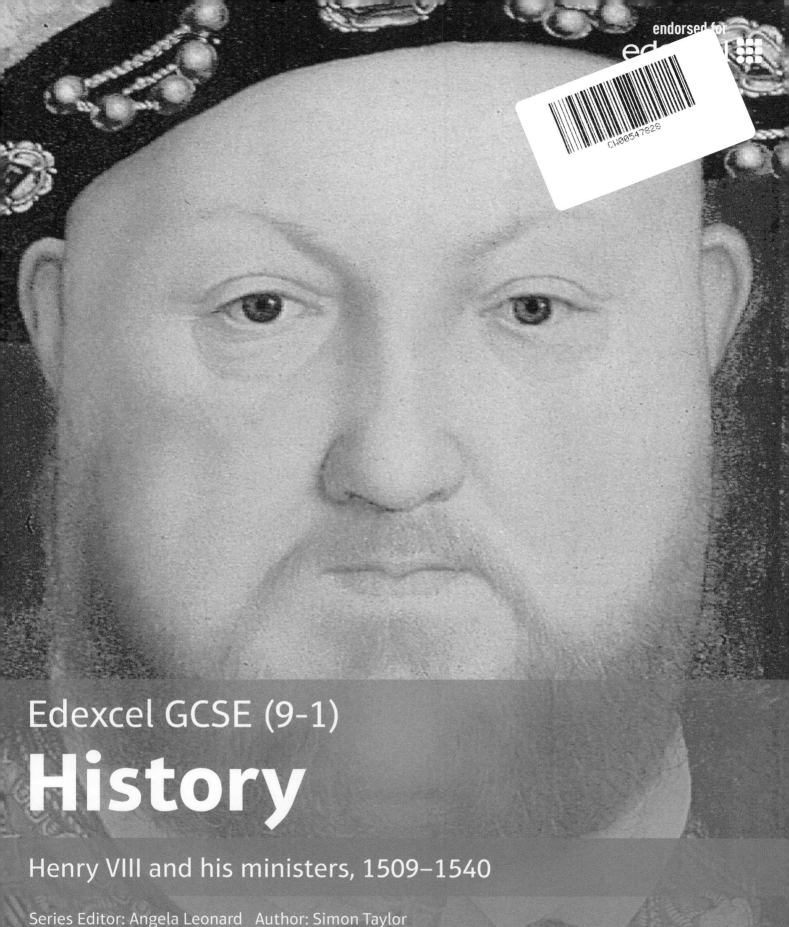

CW00547828

Edexcel GCSE (9-1)
History

Henry VIII and his ministers, 1509–1540

Series Editor: Angela Leonard   Author: Simon Taylor

ALWAYS LEARNING

PEARSON

Published by Pearson Education Limited, 80 Strand, London, WC2R 0RL.

www.pearsonschoolsandfecolleges.co.uk

Copies of official specifications for all Edexcel qualifications may be found on the website: www.edexcel.com

Text © Pearson Education Limited 2016

Series editor: Angela Leonard
Designed by Colin Tilley Loughrey, Pearson Education Limited
Typeset by Phoenix Photosetting, Chatham, Kent
Original illustrations © Pearson Education Limited
Illustrated by KJA Artists Illustration Agency and Phoenix Photosetting, Chatham, Kent.

Cover design by Colin Tilley Loughrey
Picture research by Chrissie Martin
Cover photo © Bridgeman Art Library Ltd: Palazzo Barberini, Rome, Italy

The right of Simon Taylor to be identified as author of this work has been asserted by him in accordance with the Copyright, Designs and Patents Act 1988.

First published 2016

19 18 17
10 9 8 7 6 5 4

British Library Cataloguing in Publication Data
A catalogue record for this book is available from the British Library.
ISBN 978 1 292 12725 5

Printed in the UK by CPI, UK

A note from the publisher
In order to ensure that this resource offers high-quality support for the associated Pearson qualification, it has been through a review process by the awarding body. This process confirms that this resource fully covers the teaching and learning content of the specification or part of a specification at which it is aimed. It also confirms that it demonstrates an appropriate balance between the development of subject skills, knowledge and understanding, in addition to preparation for assessment.

Endorsement does not cover any guidance on assessment activities or processes (e.g. practice questions or advice on how to answer assessment questions), included in the resource nor does it prescribe any particular approach to the teaching or delivery of a related course.

While the publishers have made every attempt to ensure that advice on the qualification and its assessment is accurate, the official specification and associated assessment guidance materials are the only authoritative source of information and should always be referred to for definitive guidance.

Pearson examiners have not contributed to any sections in this resource relevant to examination papers for which they have responsibility.

Examiners will not use endorsed resources as a source of material for any assessment set by Pearson.

Endorsement of a resource does not mean that the resource is required to achieve this Pearson qualification, nor does it mean that it is the only suitable material available to support the qualification, and any resource lists produced by the awarding body shall include this and other appropriate resources.

Websites
Pearson Education Limited is not responsible for the content of any external internet sites. It is essential for tutors to preview each website before using it in class so as to ensure that the URL is still accurate, relevant and appropriate. We suggest that tutors bookmark useful websites and consider enabling students to access them through the school/college intranet.

Contents

How to use this book

What's covered?

This book covers the British Depth study on Henry VIII and his ministers, 1509–1540. This unit makes up 20% of your GCSE course, and will be examined in Paper 2.

Depth studies cover a short period of time, and require you to know about society, people and events in detail. You need to understand how the different aspects of the period fit together and affect each other. This book also explains the different types of exam questions you will need to answer, and includes advice and example answers to help you improve.

Features

As well as a clear, detailed explanation of the key knowledge you will need, you will also find a number of features in the book:

Key terms

Where you see a word followed by an asterisk, like this: Annulment*, you will be able to find a Key Terms box on that page that explains what the word means.

> **Key term**
>
> Annulment*
> A legal term declaring that a marriage was never valid, and therefore never existed. An annulment could only be granted by the pope.

Activities

Every few pages, you'll find a box containing some activities designed to help check and embed knowledge and get you to really think about what you've studied. The activities start simple, but might get more challenging as you work through them.

Summaries and Checkpoints

At the end of each chunk of learning, the main points are summarised in a series of bullet points – great for embedding the core knowledge, and handy for revision.

Checkpoints help you to check and reflect on your learning. The Strengthen section helps you to consolidate knowledge and understanding, and check that you've grasped the basic ideas and skills. The Challenge questions push you to go beyond just understanding the information, and into evaluation and analysis of what you've studied.

Sources and Interpretations

Although source work and interpretations do not appear in Paper 2, you'll still find interesting contemporary material throughout the books, showing what people from the period said, thought or created, helping you to build your understanding of people in the past.

The book also includes extracts from the work of historians, showing how experts have interpreted the events you've been studying.

> **Interpretation 1**
>
> A leading Tudor historian, J.J Scarisbrick, outlined the significance of the rebellion in *Henry VIII*, 1997.
>
> Moreover, the rebellion might well have been an even larger convulsion than it was. It could have openly enlisted latent Yorkist sentiment and thus acquired dynastic overtones; its fire might have spread to other parts of England; there could have been Scottish intervention; there were moves towards calling for help from the emperor. Finally, Rome was ready to intervene… The crown was scarcely in greater peril… and yet, presumably because it fought for the wrong side and because it failed, the Pilgrimage has often been treated by historians as a minor, peripheral upset wrought by a few provincial conservatives, a somewhat pathetic rising which could never have succeeded against Henry's solid regime. But the truth is that, if it had wanted, it might have swamped him.

Extend your knowledge

These features contain useful additional information that adds depth to your knowledge, and to your answers. The information is closely related to the key issues in the unit, and questions are sometimes included, helping you to link the new details to the main content.

> **Extend your knowledge**
>
> **Anne's miscarriage**
> Some historians have argued that Anne gave birth to a deformed baby in 1536. If so, this would have provided Henry with further evidence of God's displeasure. It would also have raised suspicion that Anne was a witch. However, there is no real evidence to support this theory. It was probably a lie.

Exam-style questions and tips

The book also includes extra exam-style questions you can use to practise. These appear in the chapters and are accompanied by a tip to help you get started on an answer.

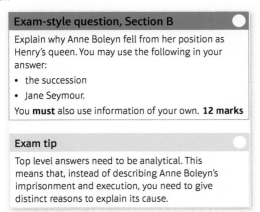

Exam-style question, Section B

Explain why Anne Boleyn fell from her position as Henry's queen. You may use the following in your answer:

- the succession
- Jane Seymour.

You **must** also use information of your own. **12 marks**

Exam tip

Top level answers need to be analytical. This means that, instead of describing Anne Boleyn's imprisonment and execution, you need to give distinct reasons to explain its cause.

Recap pages

At the end of each chapter, you'll find a page designed to help you to consolidate and reflect on the chapter as a whole. Each recap page includes a recall quiz, ideal for quickly checking your knowledge or for revision. Recap pages also include activities designed to help you summarise and analyse what you've learned, and also reflect on how each chapter links to other parts of the unit.

THINKING HISTORICALLY

These activities are designed to help you develop a better understanding of how history is constructed, and are focused on the key areas of Evidence, Interpretations, Cause & Consequence and Change & Continuity. In the British Depth Study, you will come across activities on Cause & Consequence, as this is a key focus for this unit.

The Thinking Historically approach has been developed in conjunction with Dr Arthur Chapman and the Institute of Education, UCL. It is based on research into the misconceptions that can hold students back in history.

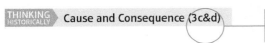

THINKING HISTORICALLY   Cause and Consequence (3c&d)   conceptual map reference

The Thinking Historically conceptual map can be found at: www.pearsonschools.co.uk/thinkinghistoricallygcse

WRITING HISTORICALLY

At the end of most chapters is a spread dedicated to helping you improve your writing skills. These include simple techniques you can use in your writing to make your answers clearer, more precise and better focused on the question you're answering.

The Writing Historically approach is based on the *Grammar for Writing* pedagogy developed by a team at the University of Exeter and popular in many English departments. Each spread uses examples from the preceding chapter, so it's relevant to what you've just been studying.

Preparing for your exams

At the back of the book, you'll find a special section dedicated to explaining and exemplifying the new Edexcel GCSE History exams. Advice on the demands of this paper, written by Angela Leonard, helps you prepare for and approach the exam with confidence. Each question type is explained through annotated sample answers at two levels, showing clearly how answers can be improved.

Pearson Progression Scale: This icon indicates the Step that a sample answer has been graded at on the Pearson Progression Scale.

This book is also available as an online ActiveBook, which can be licensed for your whole institution.

There is also an ActiveLearn Digital Service available to support delivery of this book, featuring a front-of-class version of the book, lesson plans, worksheets, exam practice PowerPoints, assessments, notes on Thinking Historically and Writing Historically, and more.

ActiveLearn
Digital Service

Timeline: Henry VIII, his wives and chief ministers

The Chief Ministers of Henry VIII

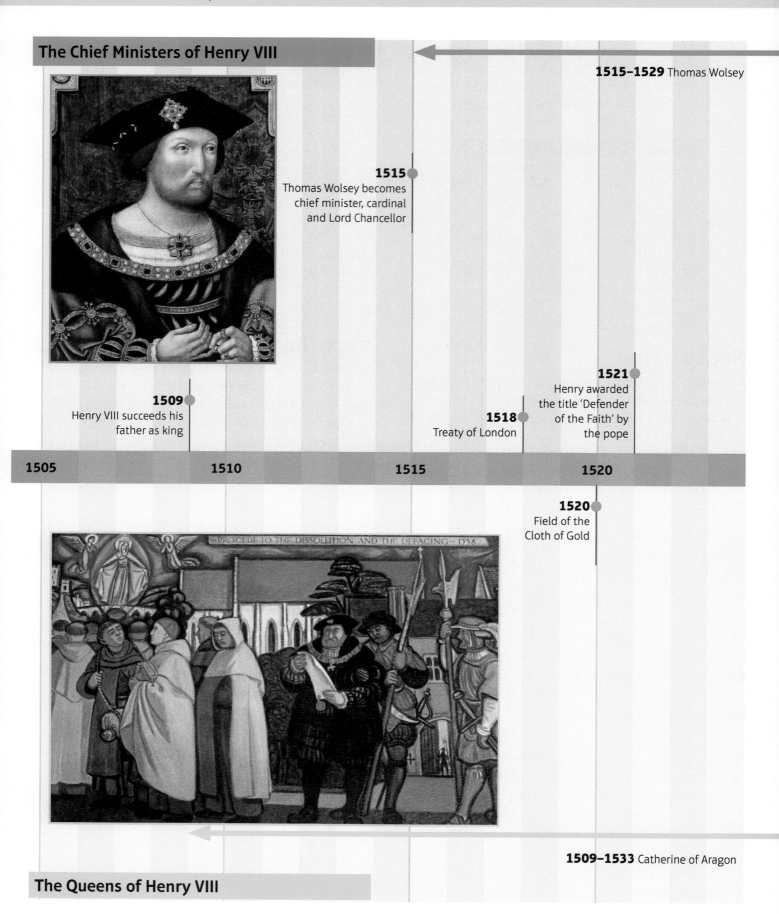

1515–1529 Thomas Wolsey

1515
Thomas Wolsey becomes chief minister, cardinal and Lord Chancellor

1521
Henry awarded the title 'Defender of the Faith' by the pope

1518
Treaty of London

1509
Henry VIII succeeds his father as king

1505	1510	1515	1520

1520
Field of the Cloth of Gold

1509–1533 Catherine of Aragon

The Queens of Henry VIII

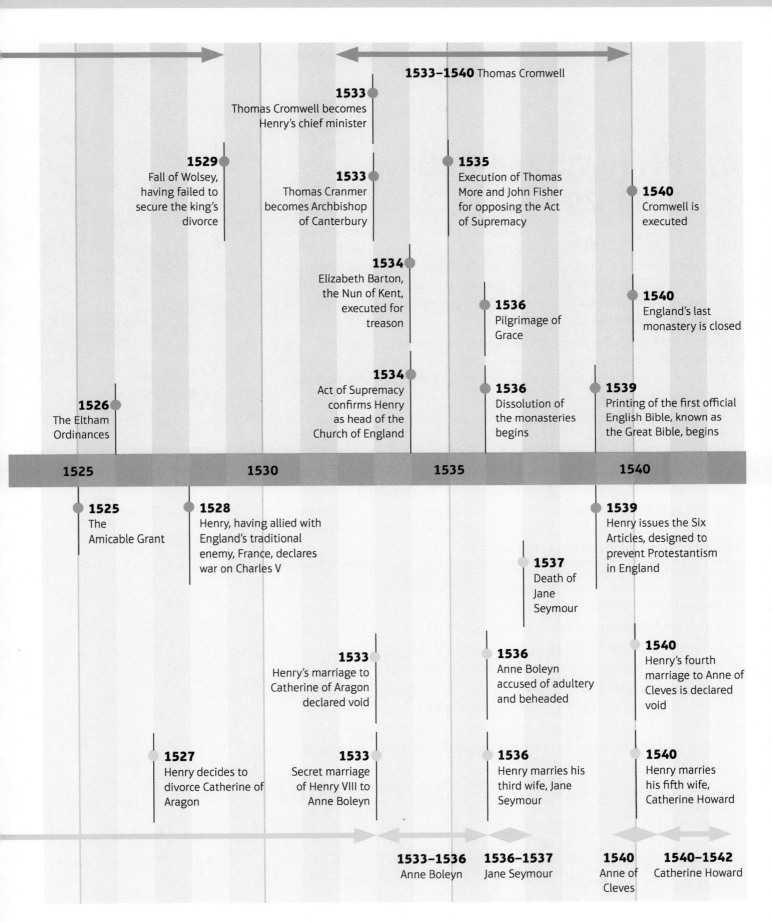

1533–1540 Thomas Cromwell

1533
Thomas Cromwell becomes Henry's chief minister

1529
Fall of Wolsey, having failed to secure the king's divorce

1533
Thomas Cranmer becomes Archbishop of Canterbury

1535
Execution of Thomas More and John Fisher for opposing the Act of Supremacy

1540
Cromwell is executed

1534
Elizabeth Barton, the Nun of Kent, executed for treason

1536
Pilgrimage of Grace

1540
England's last monastery is closed

1526
The Eltham Ordinances

1534
Act of Supremacy confirms Henry as head of the Church of England

1536
Dissolution of the monasteries begins

1539
Printing of the first official English Bible, known as the Great Bible, begins

1525	1530	1535	1540

1525
The Amicable Grant

1528
Henry, having allied with England's traditional enemy, France, declares war on Charles V

1539
Henry issues the Six Articles, designed to prevent Protestantism in England

1537
Death of Jane Seymour

1533
Henry's marriage to Catherine of Aragon declared void

1536
Anne Boleyn accused of adultery and beheaded

1540
Henry's fourth marriage to Anne of Cleves is declared void

1527
Henry decides to divorce Catherine of Aragon

1533
Secret marriage of Henry VIII to Anne Boleyn

1536
Henry marries his third wife, Jane Seymour

1540
Henry marries his fifth wife, Catherine Howard

1533–1536
Anne Boleyn

1536–1537
Jane Seymour

1540
Anne of Cleves

1540–1542
Catherine Howard

7

01 | Henry VIII and Wolsey, 1509–29

The Tudor dynasty was born on the battlefield. Henry VIII's father, Henry VII, fought and defeated King Richard III to win the throne. As a result, he found the rest of his life haunted by dangers and plots. In contrast, Henry VIII inherited the throne peacefully. His coronation was greeted with celebrations, bonfires and high hopes for a better future.

It is not hard to see why. Henry VIII was young, handsome, athletic and charming. He looked and behaved like an ideal king. For inspiration, the new king modelled himself both on the legends of King Arthur and on the latest ideas of the Renaissance.

However, Henry VIII did not forget about the pressures of ruling, nor did he underestimate what it took to be a king. Above all, he wanted war to prove himself a true knight. To make this happen, he needed help.

Thomas Wolsey had grown up with none of the advantages enjoyed by Henry, but had risen to the top through ruthlessness, ability and ambition. He knew that his right to stay at the top rested on his continuing ability to turn the whims of Henry VIII into reality. The first half of Henry's reign was, in many ways, the combined journey of these two men.

Learning outcomes

By the end of this chapter, you will:

- understand Henry VIII's character, and his aims, at the start of his reign
- know about the rise of Thomas Wolsey, Henry VIII's chief minister, and the impact of his legal, financial, land and administrative reforms
- know about foreign policy under Wolsey and the extent to which he was able to turn Henry VIII into a great European leader
- understand why Henry wanted an annulment of his marriage to Catherine of Aragon and how Wolsey's failure to secure this contributed to his downfall.

1.1 Henry VIII, Renaissance Prince

Learning outcomes

- Understand English society in 1509.
- Understand Henry VIII's character and attitudes on becoming king.

England in 1509: society and government

Henry VIII's father, Henry VII (shown in Source A), became king in 1485. Over time, Henry VII became identified with greed and repression. His son, however, was determined to be different. When Henry VIII succeeded to the throne, in 1509, he wanted to become known as a king of great wealth, prosperity and generosity.

Aged only 18 in 1509, the young king now ruled over 2.5 million people. His was a mainly rural kingdom, with most people living and working on the land. Only around 6% of the population lived in towns. The city of London was the largest and most important in the country, with 60,000 inhabitants. The next largest towns were Norwich, Bristol, Exeter, York and Coventry, but they had much smaller populations. The religion of the whole of England was Roman Catholicism – a form of Christianity followed throughout Western Europe during much of Henry VIII's reign.

The young Henry becomes king

Henry did not expect to be king. He was born the second son of Henry VII and Elizabeth of York. While his elder brother Arthur, as the Prince of Wales, went off to learn the art of government in Wales, Henry's early childhood was spent in Eltham Palace, just outside London. He was brought up with his two sisters, Margaret and Mary, under the supervision of his mother. An energetic and outgoing young boy, Henry's life changed dramatically in 1502 when his elder brother died of tuberculosis. Aged ten, Henry became the heir to the throne.

As the sole surviving male heir, Henry was moved to the royal court at Greenwich to be kept under the close and stern supervision of his father. Having already lost five out of eight children, the king felt that Henry was too precious to risk. Although the teenage prince was strong and athletic, enjoying hunting and archery, his father banned him from the dangerous sport of jousting*. This angered Henry greatly.

More surprisingly, he was also denied any role in governing the kingdom, despite being intelligent and having studied with leading scholars. Traditionally, the Prince of Wales was sent to the Welsh Marches (English land along the Welsh border) to learn how to govern. Following Arthur's death, Henry VII had no wish to send another son off to a tough part of the country to build experience. As a result, on his father's death in 1509, Henry VIII was largely untrained in the skills needed to rule as king.

Source A

A portrait of the 48-year-old Henry VII by an unknown artist, painted in 1505, four years before his death.

Key term

Jousting*

A sporting contest where two opponents on horseback try to knock the other to the ground with a lance.

Source B

Henry VIII painted in 1520 by an unknown artist.

Source C

A leading English baron, William Blount, wrote to the famous scholar Erasmus shortly after Henry's coronation on 27 May 1509.

When you know what a hero the king now shows himself, how wisely he behaves, what a lover he is of justice and goodness, what affection he bears to the learned, I will venture that you will need no wings to make you fly to behold this new and auspicious star. If you could see how all the world here is rejoicing in the possession of so great a prince, how his life is all their desire, you could not contain your tears of joy.

Key terms

Accession*

Becoming king or queen.

Betrothed*

A formal engagement that could not be easily broken.

Royal progress*

A royal tour of the kingdom. It was important for the king to travel widely so he could be seen and admired by the people. It was also a way of meeting and forming relationships with local leaders.

This lack of experience did not worry Henry VIII. His accession* was greeted with genuine enthusiasm across the country. Source C gives an idea of the countless compliments given to the new king. By comparing the two portraits of father and son in Sources A and B, this popular reaction is not hard to understand. Henry VIII appears open and handsome, in great contrast to his father, who looks tired and suspicious, with a shrewd sideways glance, his hands tightly gripped.

Henry VIII also took steps to immediately distance himself from his father. For example, he ordered the arrest of the two ministers most closely identified with Henry VII's hated financial policies.

Henry married Catherine of Aragon, a princess of Spain. Catherine had come to England in 1501 and married Prince Arthur; but, following Arthur's death, she was betrothed* to Henry in 1503. When they married, in 1509, it strengthened an important alliance with Spain and Henry gained a wife he was genuinely fond of.

However, the new king still had a lot to thank his father for. He inherited a stable, well-governed kingdom, a group of experienced advisers and a wealthy country.

Henry VIII's character

Henry was a powerful athlete and excelled in things like archery and wrestling. While out hunting, Henry could tire out eight to ten horses before tiring himself. However, his greatest passion was jousting. With his father no longer around to prevent him, Henry jousted regularly. Surviving score cards show that his jousting skills were truly brilliant.

Henry knew how to have fun and pursued pleasure above all things, even in affairs of the state. Source D gives an idea of how Henry spent his time on one royal progress* around England. Those who met the young king found him friendly, affectionate and generous.

Henry was a true Renaissance* man. Along with his athletic ability and his courage, he was gifted in many areas, priding himself on his intellect and enjoying the company of leading scholars. Henry spoke French, Spanish and Latin, and was a talented musician and composer. To entertain visitors from the French court, for example, he once played on every musical instrument available. He also possessed a fine singing voice and his elegance in dancing was often noted. The king also loved to dress in fine clothes and cover himself with jewels.

Henry's views on sovereignty and monarchy

Henry was also a deeply religious man: as a Roman Catholic, he attended church services and gave charity to the poor on a daily basis.

However, he still had his faults. Henry had a big ego and believed his opinions were the only thing that mattered. Henry would have seen this as natural as, like all kings of the period, he believed he had been appointed directly by God. This was called **divine right**.

So Henry was stubborn, and his advisers found it very difficult to change his mind once it was set. Thomas Wolsey, Henry's chief adviser from early in his reign, claimed he spent hours on his knees trying to change the young king's mind on important state matters. He usually failed.

Tudor society

Henry's England was hierarchical – which meant that you were ranked in society based on your wealth and social status. There was only very limited opportunities to move up the social ladder. It was the commonly-held view that God was at the top of this 'Great Chain of Being,' as shown in Figure 1.1. Figure 1.2 shows the main ranks into which society was divided. Everyone was expected to know their place and show respect to those above them. Most people accepted this, although, as will be seen later, a few talented individuals, like Wolsey and Cromwell, were able to defy the odds and move up the social ladder. However, despite the social differences, most people in England shared the same religion. They followed a common Christian faith and attended Roman Catholic Church services.

Source D

From *The Union of the Two Noble and Illustre [Illustrious] Families of Lancaster and York* by Edward Hall, published in 1542. In this extract, Hall describes Henry's activities while on a royal progress in 1511.

Henry exercised himself in shooting, singing, dancing, wrestling, casting of the bar, playing at the recorders, flute and virginals [musical instrument], and in setting of songs, making of ballads and did set two godly Masses, every of them of five parts, which were sung oftentimes in his chapel and afterwards in divers other places. And when he came to Woking, there were kept both jousts and tourneys. The rest of his time was spent in hunting, hawking and shooting.

Key term

Renaissance*

A revival of European art and culture, based upon the ideas of ancient Greece and Rome. It also included a new appreciation of learning. The Renaissance started in northern Italy in the 14th century and then spread throughout Europe.

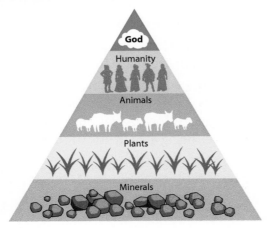

Figure 1.1 The 'Great Chain of Being'.

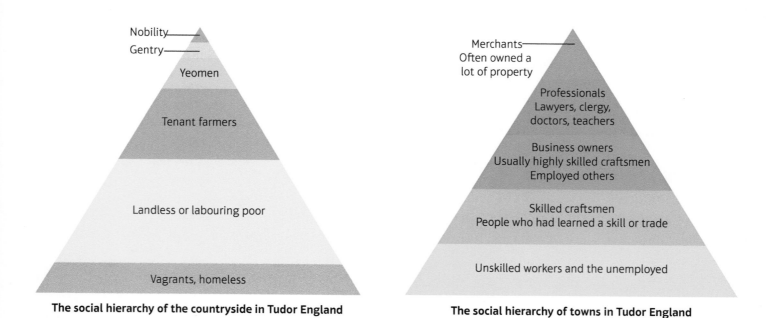

The social hierarchy of the countryside in Tudor England

The social hierarchy of towns in Tudor England

Figure 1.2 The social structure of Tudor England.

Ruling a small kingdom, like England, was a personal business. The table below shows how Henry VIII ruled.

	Key features of Henry VIII's government
The king	Ruled the country and made all the important decisions on foreign and domestic policy, including when to go to war and when parliament should be called. Settled disputes between nobles and made appointments to important religious and political posts.
Royal Household	A mixed membership of nobles and servants ensured that the king was provided with food, clothing and spiritual guidance. It also played an important role in government. In the rooms of the Royal Household, the king held audiences, met with advisers and made important decisions.
Privy Chamber	Part of the Royal Household, with both domestic and political responsibilities. It was made up of a small group of the king's closest noble friends. They looked after his personal needs, as well as providing entertainment. These gentlemen had huge opportunities to informally influence the king on matters of policy. The Privy Chamber was headed by the Groom of the Stool.
Royal Council	A group of advisers chosen by the king and selected mainly from the nobility and Church. They provided guidance on policy, as well as handling routine matters of state.
Court	A body of people made up of the monarch's key servants, advisers and friends. Drawn mainly from members of the nobility, they were known as **courtiers**. They lived in, or near, the same palace or house as the king, entertaining him and his visiting guests. The size and splendour of the assembled court allowed the king to display his wealth and power. Being able to attend court required the monarch's permission.
Parliament	Made up of the **House of Lords** (which included bishops) and the **House of Commons**. Its main job was to pass laws requested by the king and to approve new taxes for him.
Justices of the Peace	Large landowners who kept law and order in their local areas (JPs for short).

Henry created his own personal style of government. In particular, he chose to rely on two groups for advice and guidance: the Royal Council and the Privy Chamber. A few years into his rule, Henry also started carrying out a great deal of his work through a single trusted **chief minister**. The first of these was Thomas Wolsey.

Henry's personal style did not include paperwork or administration. Unlike his father, who had paid very close attention to all aspects of governing the kingdom, routine tasks bored Henry. He was content to let others look after the everyday process of government.

Extend your knowledge

The Groom of the Stool
The Groom of the Stool was officially in charge of cleaning the king's bottom! This post was highly prized because of the close physical contact with the king. It was not seen as demeaning in Tudor times.

Henry's attitude to kingship

Henry had a very clear vision for his kingship. He wanted to model his rule on the great Renaissance monarchies of France and Spain. In these monarchies, the king was a towering figure, with a dazzling court that showed the king's majesty and celebrated the latest ideas in the arts, culture and learning.

Henry also looked to England's own past for inspiration. In particular, he dreamed about repeating the heroic victories achieved by English kings over the French. Henry had grown up listening to the stories of the legendary King Arthur and the Knights of the Round Table. For Henry, kingship also involved performing brave deeds, from jousts to actual war, as well as being skilled in the art of courtly love*.

Key term

Courtly love*
A form of elite entertainment, in which noble gentlemen attempted to win the hearts of women through songs, poetry and quests. In return, the sought-after lady was expected to pretend they were uninterested.

Henry VIII's aims as monarch

Based on Henry's attitude to kingship, his aims as a monarch can be summarised by five main points.

1 Henry wanted to decide on England's policies and dictate this to his ministers.
2 Henry wanted to achieve glorious victories in battle abroad.
3 Henry wanted to create a magnificent royal court, through art, architecture, dress and entertainment.
4 Henry wanted to attract great men to his court, such as important scholars and artists.
5 Henry wanted to perform the traditional duties of a monarch, including: maintaining law and order, being a good servant to the Church, and having a son to continue the royal line.

Activities ?

1 In groups, discuss the following statement: 'In 1509, England's new king had everything going for him'. To help you explore this, use the table on the next page to rank the strengths and weaknesses of Henry VIII's monarchy. Give each factor a score out of ten for importance.
2 Discuss the question in groups, using the rankings that you have given to each strength and weakness to help you.
3 Write a short paragraph, explaining whether you agree or disagree with the statement and why.

Exam-style question, Section B

Describe two key features of Henry VIII's government.
4 marks

Exam tip

Make sure you add supporting information for both features.

The strengths and weaknesses of Henry VIII's monarchy in 1509

Strengths	Weaknesses
• He was popular with the people of England, as he looked the part of a great king.	• He had little experience of government.
• He inherited a rich country from his father.	• He had little desire to get involved in the day-to-day business of governing England.
• England was stable, with an established system of government.	• His attitude to kingship was simplistic and partly based on heroic legends.
• He loved his wife, Catherine of Aragon, and she had important foreign connections in Spain.	• He wanted England to go to war as soon as possible, so he could prove himself a true, heroic knight.
• He had a team of experienced advisers around him.	• He had a large ego that was difficult to manage.
• He had ambition to become a great Renaissance king.	• He liked high-risk sports such as jousting, which could threaten his health.

Summary

- Henry's England was mainly rural, with few large towns. The people of England were divided into different ranks, but united by a common Christian faith – Roman Catholicism.
- Henry VIII's accession to the throne in 1509 was greeted with great enthusiasm. Henry VIII looked the part of a glorious king: he was tall, handsome and strong.
- Henry VIII had firm ideas about what type of king he wanted to be. He modelled himself on the great Renaissance courts of Europe, as well as the heroic kings of England's past.
- First and foremost, he wanted to prove himself in battle. He also wanted to promote the arts, culture and learning.
- Henry did not want to get involved in the day-to-day affairs of government, preferring to leave these tasks to trusted ministers in the Royal Council. Instead, most of his time was given to pleasure.

Checkpoint

Strengthen

S1 Describe the Royal Council and the Privy Chamber.

S2 Describe four features of English society in 1509.

S3 Why was Henry described as a 'Renaissance Prince'?

Challenge

C1 Why did Henry's accession to the throne in 1509 create so much excitement? Think of at least three reasons.

C2 Did Henry have the right character and outlook for ruling England? Explore his strengths and weaknesses.

C3 What methods existed for people to influence the way Henry governed England?

If you are not confident about answering these questions, form a group with other students to discuss the answers.

1.2 The rise of Wolsey and his policies

Learning outcomes

- Understand the reasons for Wolsey's rise to power.
- Understand Wolsey's main reforms in England.

Reasons for Wolsey's rise to power

Thomas Wolsey became England's most senior official during the first half of Henry VIII's reign. He was charming and gifted, and he dominated the country's legal, financial and administrative system following his appointment as Lord Chancellor* in 1515. As Lord Chancellor, Wolsey was the king's chief minister and main adviser on all things.

Wolsey was also one of England's most important churchmen (as Archbishop of York* and then a cardinal*). He was also skilled in building relationships with other powerful countries.

Wolsey built palaces and gained a fortune second only to the king himself, which showed how great his status was in Tudor England. Quite simply, Henry's chief minister lived like a king. Given Henry's own ego, this is surprising enough, but Thomas Wolsey also had the most unlikely of backgrounds. He was the son of an Ipswich butcher.

As seen previously, Tudor England was hierarchical. Everyone had their place in society, and those at the bottom were expected to stay there. However, Wolsey became an exception to this rule. His father, a relatively wealthy butcher and cattle dealer, provided his son with an excellent education, allowing him to enter Oxford University to study to become a priest. This was one of the few ways ambitious young men without a noble background could advance in the world.

Wolsey was very intelligent and made the most of this opportunity – gaining his degree when he was only 15 years old. Wolsey became his college's treasurer in Oxford and used his new position to undertake a huge college rebuilding programme, showing the ambition and arrogance that would later become his trademark.

Wolsey rose even further when Henry VIII became king. His appointment as **Royal Almoner** (in charge of giving charity to the poor) in 1509 made him a member of the Royal Council. The ambitious priest now had access to Henry, and the opportunity to build a personal relationship with the king using his charm, wit and gift for flattery.

Wolsey was also lucky. The young king preferred pleasure over administration. Wolsey encouraged this, and carved out a role carrying out all the tedious tasks Henry wanted to avoid.

Key terms

Lord Chancellor*

The most important post in Henry VIII's government, responsible for advising the king on all matters.

Archbishop of York*

The second most important religious appointment in England, after the Archbishop of Canterbury.

Cardinal*

A senior leader in the Roman Catholic Church.

Source A

Thomas Wolsey, dressed in the scarlet robes of a cardinal. Painted by Sampson Strong, 1610.

Wolsey was also fortunate that Henry disliked many of the advisers inherited from his father. He saw them as old, boring and cautious, and in the first few years of his reign, many were arrested or retired. So Wolsey was in the right place at the right time for rapid promotion.

Wolsey's 'big break' came in 1512. Henry needed someone to organise an army for war with France. This was a complex task with the potential for disaster, so few wanted the job – but Wolsey took it on. He worked hard, was ruthless with anyone who stood in his way, and successfully delivered a well-equipped and well-supplied army to France in 1513. Henry now saw Wolsey as the man who could fulfil his will quickly and efficiently, and he was soon given much more power. Wolsey's appointment as Lord Chancellor in 1515 was particularly important, as it gave him the top position in Henry's government.

As well as gaining influence with Henry as a member of his government, Wolsey also gained status and power through the Church. By 1515, he was Bishop of Lincoln, Archbishop of York and a cardinal. Wolsey engineered his appointment as **Papal Legate** in 1518. A Papal Legate represented the pope* in a foreign country so, by being the Papal Legate in England, Wolsey outranked all of the other clergy in the English Church.

Key term

Pope*

The spiritual leader of the Roman Catholic Church, based in Rome.

People at the time recognised Wolsey's great power, and he began to be referred to as an ***Alter Rex***, or 'second king'. Henry respected and trusted Wolsey, so he allowed this comparison. It was, however, the king who ultimately decided on the most important matters of state and he could, of course, overrule Wolsey.

Activity ?

Pick out three key moments from Wolsey's rise to power. Explain your choices.

Interpretation 1

Historian J.J. Scarisbrick analyses Wolsey and Henry VIII's relationship in this extract, from *Henry VIII* (1997).

For much of his career as Chancellor, it was Wolsey who alone guided English affairs. His quick, strong hands grasped everything because Henry seemed unable, or unwilling, to make the smallest decision himself. Who shall attend upon the Princess Mary? What shall he reply to the regent of the Netherlands' request to visit England? Shall the law courts be closed because of the outbreak of sweating sickness? [A sometimes fatal illness causing sweating, shivers and dizziness] And so on. All these Wolsey had to decide for him, for they were problems which this apparently helpless man, for all his bluster and swagger, could not resolve.

Life at the top

Wolsey lived like a king. As a result of his multiple jobs, appointed by both king and the Church, Wolsey gained a huge fortune. Being the Archbishop of York alone gave him an income of £3,000 per year (nearly £1 million today). He was ten times richer than his nearest rival (aside from the king).

With his wealth, he built the palaces of York House and Hampton Court for himself, and used these to entertain the English and European elite on a grand scale. He was supported by a household of 500 servants – equal in size to the king's own Royal Household.

Wolsey funded artists and musicians. His favourite project was the creation of Cardinal College in Oxford (now known as Christ Church). Such spending had an important political role. It inspired awe and envy, and showed that Wolsey was an important man.

Wolsey enjoyed this magnificent lifestyle. He had a huge personality and enjoyed showing off his new riches. He was charming and entertaining, especially gifted in the skills of flattery. However, there was also a dark side to Wolsey. He was ruthless with anyone who threatened his position, and he therefore became deeply feared and hated. Opponents to Wolsey would be jailed in the Tower of London, or financially ruined through expensive lawsuits.

Wolsey's reforms

What did Wolsey do with the power and influence he had so carefully worked for? While his main focus was always foreign policy, because of the importance Henry VIII placed upon it (see pages 21–27), he also dealt with issues at home in England. However, he was not always successful.

Justice

As Lord Chancellor, Wolsey was responsible for the legal system in England. However, it was flawed, delivering slow, expensive and often unfair justice. Verdicts often favoured those with the most money and influence.

Wolsey wanted to tackle this problem. Soon after being appointed, he sent out a clear signal that no one was to be above the law. For example, in 1516, Henry Percy, the Earl of Northumberland, and one of the heroes of the 1513 Battle of the Spurs (see page 21), was sent to prison for breaking the law.

Wolsey's main method for getting fairer justice was to strengthen the court of the **Star Chamber**, which was a royal court set up by Henry VII to give out justice on the king's behalf. It was staffed by members of the Royal Council. Wolsey secured a fairer justice system in many different ways, shown in Figure 1.3.

Although Wolsey tried to secure a fairer justice system during his time as Lord Chancellor, he was still criticised. Rather than being seen as a champion of those without money or influence, some felt that his main motivation was to get revenge on the upper classes, who had often treated him badly because of his humble origins.

Wolsey was also prepared to use his position to punish those he held a grudge against. For example, as a young priest, Wolsey had been humiliated by Sir Amyas Paulet, who had had him placed in the stocks. When he became Lord Chancellor, Wolsey summoned Paulet to the Star Chamber on a made-up charge. Wolsey then refused to see Paulet, and made him come to the court every day for five years or risk losing all his property.

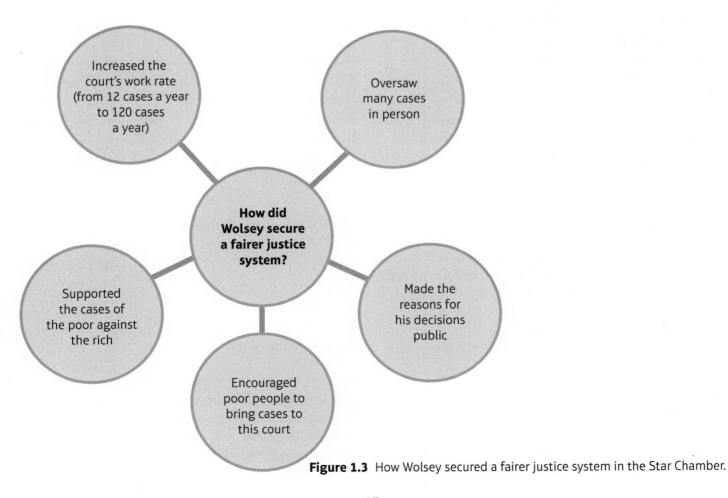

Figure 1.3 How Wolsey secured a fairer justice system in the Star Chamber.

Such actions inevitably built up resentment against Wolsey among the higher classes. Later, as Wolsey's time increasingly became tied up with foreign problems, a large backlog of cases built up in the Star Chamber, meaning very few were ever resolved.

Enclosures

Enclosure – the practice of individual landowners fencing off land for profitable sheep rearing – was being blamed for poverty in rural areas. Enclosure could lead to farmers being forced off their land and the removal of the common areas where villagers could graze their animals. Many people associated enclosure with greed and selfishness, because it meant ordinary people had less land on which to graze their animals.

Wolsey tried to find a solution to this problem, partly out of genuine concern for the poor, but also as another way he could attack the wealthy. In 1517, he set up an inquiry to investigate where land had been enclosed without proper permission. This led to over 260 court cases being brought against landowners. In an age when very few people went to court, this was a huge number.

Unsurprisingly, Wolsey's actions increased his unpopularity among the wealthy landowners of England. In 1523, angry landowners in parliament forced Wolsey to call a halt to any further investigations into enclosed land. In the long term, Wolsey's stand against enclosure achieved very little. Enclosure continued to take place, and rural poverty remained a problem.

Finance

The greatest challenge facing Wolsey at home was money. Henry wanted to follow an aggressive foreign policy to prove himself to be the greatest king in Europe, but this was expensive. Henry's normal average yearly income was £110,000, and this was not enough to win wars abroad. As Henry's chief minister, Wolsey was expected to come up with solutions, and he soon realised that the existing system of **direct taxation** was no longer working.

Direct taxation traditionally demanded that, when called upon by parliament, each community had to pay the Crown a percentage of their moveable goods* – one fifteenth of the value in rural areas, and one tenth for urban areas, like towns and cities. This was known as the

fifteenths and tenths. But the valuations were based on estimates from the 14th century and so were very outdated. The amount collected under this system was predictable and reliable, but it wasn't enough.

Key term

Moveable goods*

Possessions that could be moved from one location to another, such as furniture, household items and livestock. Land and buildings were not moveable, and so did not count under the value of moveable goods.

Wolsey's solution was to improve the system of direct taxation with the **subsidy**. This was an additional tax based on an up-to-date assessment of a person's income, with commissioners being sent out across the country to ensure valuations were accurate. The tax was set up in such a way that, the greater a person's income, the more tax they paid. This is very similar to how income tax is calculated in England today.

Wolsey saw the subsidy as a success because it more accurately taxed people based on what they could afford to pay. So the rich paid the most tax. Above all, the tax worked. Between 1513 and 1516, for example, the subsidy raised £170,000, while the fifteenths and tenths raised only £90,000. During his time as Lord Chancellor, Wolsey collected four subsidies, each one helping to pay for the war in France.

Wolsey also made use of other pre-existing methods of raising money.

The main sources of revenue raised by Wolsey, 1513–29	
Tax	Amount raised
Subsidy	£322,000
Forced loans	£260,000
Clerical taxation	£240,000
Fifteenths and tenths	£118,000

While the total amounts were impressive and ensured there was never a financial crisis in Henry's early reign, they still could not keep pace with Henry's spending. Around £1.4 million went on fighting wars between 1511 and 1525. Also, the heavy rates of taxation were very unpopular.

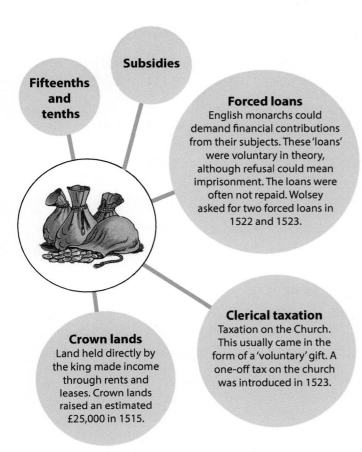

Figure 1.4 The ways in which Wolsey raised money.

Subsidies

Fifteenths and tenths

Forced loans
English monarchs could demand financial contributions from their subjects. These 'loans' were voluntary in theory, although refusal could mean imprisonment. The loans were often not repaid. Wolsey asked for two forced loans in 1522 and 1523.

Crown lands
Land held directly by the king made income through rents and leases. Crown lands raised an estimated £25,000 in 1515.

Clerical taxation
Taxation on the Church. This usually came in the form of a 'voluntary' gift. A one-off tax on the church was introduced in 1523.

The Amicable Grant, 1525

Reasons for the Amicable Grant

The king of France was spectacularly defeated by Charles V and captured in 1525 (see page 25). Because of this, Henry VIII wanted to seize the opportunity to invade France when it was at its most vulnerable. England had used up most of its money in a failed invasion of France in 1523 (see page 25). So, having already demanded various forced loans and subsidies in the period 1522–24, Wolsey looked for new ways to raise funds. His solution was to impose a new direct tax without gaining the approval of parliament.

This was a potentially dangerous move. One of parliament's main roles was to make sure the king did not tax the country too hard: both the fifteenths and tenths and subsidy were all granted by parliament. If parliament was ignored, or not consulted on matters of taxation, there was the risk of rebellion against the king's rule.

The Amicable Grant demanded that priests pay one third of their income and everyone else one sixth as a tax. People were given just ten weeks to find the money.

Reactions to the Amicable Grant

As the commissioners went out to collect the tax, they were greeted with anger; and many people simply refused to pay, saying they had no money. A full scale revolt broke out in Suffolk in May 1525, when 10,000 men met in the main market town of Lavenham. Once there, they expressed loyalty to the king, but made it clear that they also wanted the Crown to be made aware of their anger. The rebels were met by a small force under the Dukes of Norfolk and Suffolk, who negotiated the rebels' surrender.

- The impact of these protests was far reaching. It was the first significant rebellion of Henry's reign.
- Henry claimed that he was unaware of the tax and ordered its collection to be stopped.
- Wolsey was humiliated and accepted complete responsibility for the failure of the taxation. Wolsey's unpopularity increased.
- Henry started to doubt the talents of his chief minister. It marked the beginning of the end for Wolsey.
- No further taxation was attempted by Wolsey again.
- Henry's wish to attack France had to be abandoned – instead, he sought peace.
- The leaders of the protest movement in Suffolk were pardoned.

Source B

From *The Union of the Two Noble and Illustre Families of Lancaster and York* by Edward Hall, published in 1542. This extract tells how Henry abandoned the Amicable Grant.

The king was sore moved that his subjects were so stirred... he thought it touched his honour that his council should attempt such a doubtful matter in his name... Then the king said, I will no more of this trouble: Let letters be sent to all shires, that this matter may no more be spoken of, I will pardon all them that have denied the demand, openly or secretly. Then all the lords kneeled down, and heartedly thanked the king.

Cause and Consequence (3a&b)

The might of human agency

1   Describe to your partner a situation where things did not work out as you had intended. Then explain how you would have done things differently to make the situation as you would have wanted. Your partner will then tell the group about that situation and whether they think that your alternative actions would have had the desired effect.

2   **a**   Write down what Wolsey's aims were for the Amicable Grant.

   b   Write down what Wolsey's actions were.

   c   To what extent was Wolsey successful?

   d   Make a spider diagram: write Wolsey's actions in the middle and then add as many consequences of his actions as possible around them. Think about the long-term consequences as well as the immediate ones.

   e   How important were the consequences of Wolsey's actions for his own future?

3   To what extent are individuals in control of the history they helped to create? Explain your answer in a paragraph, with reference to specific historical examples from both this topic and others.

The Eltham Ordinances

In 1526, Wolsey turned to reforming both the domestic and political aspects of the king's household.

As a result of the hundreds of people attending court on a daily basis, Henry's palaces were dirty, bad behaviour was common and money was spent without thought. To tackle this, Wolsey drew up a detailed list of rules known as the **Eltham Ordinances**. Many of the measures he proposed were long overdue, and some are listed below.

- Servants who were sick or not needed were laid off.
- The number of people who were allowed expenses for things like food, drink, fuel and lodgings was cut.
- Meals were at set times, instead of constant.
- Dogs were banned to promote cleanliness, although the ladies were allowed to keep their small spaniels.

In total, the Eltham Ordinances were 79 chapters long.

Within the ordinances, Wolsey also passed reforms to change the King's Privy Chamber. Wolsey reduced the Gentlemen of the Chamber from 12 to six men. The public reason for this was to save money. Wolsey's other main concern, though, was to side-line his political rivals. As soon as this reduction was carried out, Wolsey lost interest in applying the other domestic measures.

Summary

- For 15 years, Wolsey dominated Henry's government. He rose from humble origins, and was hard working.
- The nobility did not like Wolsey because of his humble origins, but he became too dangerous to criticise.
- Wolsey also did not forget his origins, and helped the lower classes by taking a stand against enclosure and increasing access to fair justice in the Star Chamber.
- For Henry VIII, Wolsey's greatest contribution to domestic politics must have been expanding government revenue through taxation.
- His position became weaker because he abused his power: his policies and actions created many enemies.

Checkpoint

Strengthen

S1 Describe how Wolsey attempted to make justice fairer.

S2 Describe the range of reactions to the Amicable Grant.

Challenge

C1 In what ways did Wolsey's humble origins shape the type of policies he pursued as chief minister?

C2 Why did Wolsey became so unpopular with many in the nobility?

If you are not confident answering these questions, list the pros and cons of all of Wolsey's domestic reforms to help you.

1.3 Wolsey's foreign policy

Learning outcomes

- Understand Wolsey's main foreign policy aims.
- Understand Wolsey's successes and failures in foreign policy.

Timeline

Foreign affairs, 1512–25

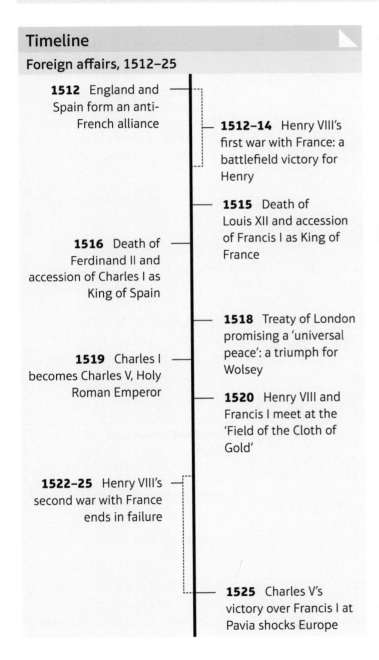

1512 England and Spain form an anti-French alliance

1512–14 Henry VIII's first war with France: a battlefield victory for Henry

1515 Death of Louis XII and accession of Francis I as King of France

1516 Death of Ferdinand II and accession of Charles I as King of Spain

1518 Treaty of London promising a 'universal peace': a triumph for Wolsey

1519 Charles I becomes Charles V, Holy Roman Emperor

1520 Henry VIII and Francis I meet at the 'Field of the Cloth of Gold'

1522–25 Henry VIII's second war with France ends in failure

1525 Charles V's victory over Francis I at Pavia shocks Europe

Henry's European rivals

Young Henry VIII was first and foremost a warrior. His favourite hobbies of jousting, archery and hunting all had the purpose of preparing him for battle. Henry dreamed of military glory and, ultimately, this meant only one thing: the re-conquest of France. However, in reality, England did not have the population and resources to compete with the European superpowers of France and the Habsburg* Empire (see Figure 1.5).

Key term

Habsburg*

The Habsburgs were a royal Catholic family that ruled Spain during Henry VIII's reign. Many branches of this family also ruled other parts of Europe, including Austria.

The difficulties in achieving English glory were made clear to Henry when he invaded France in 1512. It ended in humiliation. His army failed because of drunkenness and disease.

Henry launched a second campaign in 1513. This time, Henry captured the towns of Therouanne and Tournai, and defeated the French army at the **Battle of the Spurs**. Henry could boast about this victory as a success. However, in reality, the two towns were of little value and the battle was only a minor one. Also, this second campaign emptied the king's treasury.

However, by 1514, Wolsey had established himself as Henry's chief diplomat and became the man who had to balance his master's dreams with reality. For the next 15 years, Wolsey was the driving force behind England's foreign policy.

The major players Henry had to contend with in Europe were Francis I, the king of France from 1515, and Charles I, the king of Spain from 1516.

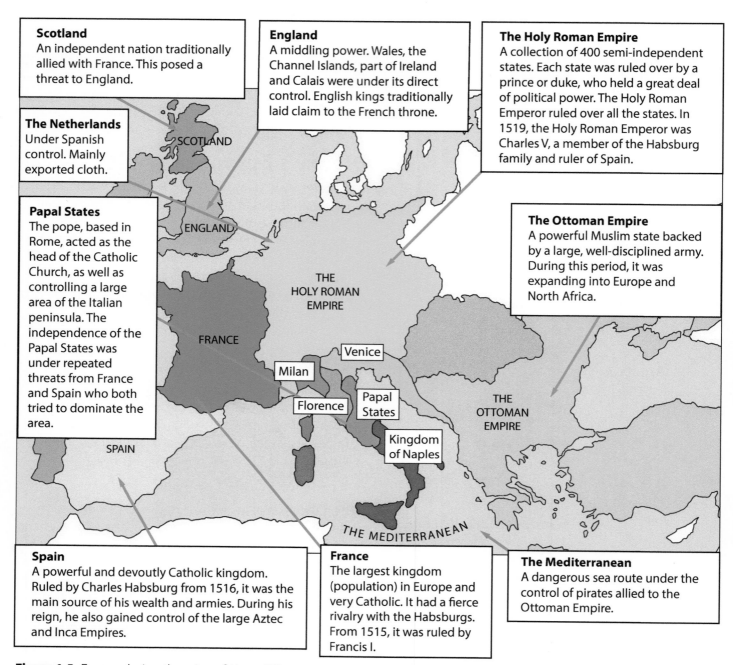

Scotland
An independent nation traditionally allied with France. This posed a threat to England.

The Netherlands
Under Spanish control. Mainly exported cloth.

Papal States
The pope, based in Rome, acted as the head of the Catholic Church, as well as controlling a large area of the Italian peninsula. The independence of the Papal States was under repeated threats from France and Spain who both tried to dominate the area.

England
A middling power. Wales, the Channel Islands, part of Ireland and Calais were under its direct control. English kings traditionally laid claim to the French throne.

The Holy Roman Empire
A collection of 400 semi-independent states. Each state was ruled over by a prince or duke, who held a great deal of political power. The Holy Roman Emperor ruled over all the states. In 1519, the Holy Roman Emperor was Charles V, a member of the Habsburg family and ruler of Spain.

The Ottoman Empire
A powerful Muslim state backed by a large, well-disciplined army. During this period, it was expanding into Europe and North Africa.

SCOTLAND

ENGLAND

THE HOLY ROMAN EMPIRE

FRANCE

Venice

Milan

Florence

Papal States

Kingdom of Naples

THE OTTOMAN EMPIRE

SPAIN

THE MEDITERRANEAN

Spain
A powerful and devoutly Catholic kingdom. Ruled by Charles Habsburg from 1516, it was the main source of his wealth and armies. During his reign, he also gained control of the large Aztec and Inca Empires.

France
The largest kingdom (population) in Europe and very Catholic. It had a fierce rivalry with the Habsburgs. From 1515, it was ruled by Francis I.

The Mediterranean
A dangerous sea route under the control of pirates allied to the Ottoman Empire.

Figure 1.5 Europe during the reign of Henry VIII.

Like Henry, Francis and Charles were young, bright and ambitious, but also far more powerful than Henry. It was the rivalry between France and Spain that dominated foreign affairs. They had conflicting claims over various parts of Europe. Because of this, Spain and France often fought over these disputed territories.

Spain was an attractive ally for England over France. Henry was married to Catherine of Aragon, Charles I's aunt; and England's economy relied on the Netherlands, as they had a very strong cloth market (also under Spanish control). Not only was France a traditional enemy, but Francis I was so similar to Henry in terms of character that a rivalry was inevitable, as shown in Source A.

Source A

A conversation about Francis I, between Henry VIII and the Venetian ambassador, who had just passed through France.

'Is he as tall as I am?'

'Yes, Your Grace, just about.'

'And as broad across the shoulders?'

'Not quite.'

'Ah! And his legs?'

'Rather thin, Your Majesty.'

'Look at mine!' And the King opened the folds of his tunic to reveal his thighs. 'And my calves too are every bit as beautiful.'

This rivalry was confirmed when Francis I won a spectacular victory against Spanish forces in northern Italy in 1515 and seized Milan. Francis was in the thick of the fighting. Henry was deeply jealous and also worried about his rival's growing power. Wolsey immediately tried to gather allies in Europe against France, but his efforts achieved very little.

Shortly after, Francis made peace with Spain and then with the Holy Roman Empire* – leaving England standing alone against the main powers of Europe.

Activity ?

The year is 1515. Wolsey has just become chief minister. Henry wants to be briefed on the current international situation. He is particularly interested in finding out about his main rivals, threats on the continent and opportunities.

Imagine you are Wolsey. Plan and deliver a presentation to be given to Henry on the international situation in 1515.

Key term

Holy Roman Empire*

A group of different states and kingdoms covering a large area of central Europe. Although each state had its own ruler, the leaders of the seven largest states elected a Holy Roman Emperor to rule over them.

Wolsey's successes and failures in foreign policy

Wolsey and Henry's foreign policy aims

I want to create a better relationship with both France and the Habsburg Empire. This will make sure that England is not left diplomatically isolated, with France and the Habsburg Empire becoming allies against us.

I hope it will provide opportunities for playing one power (France) against the other (Habsburg Empire) to England's advantage.

I want to provide opportunities for Henry to gain military glory in battle. Although I frequently warn Henry against expensive wars, I know that Henry wants glory on the battlefield and my own position depends on serving the king's interests.

If Henry is seen as the European peacemaker, it will give him the international prestige he wants; but it is also a sensible policy given that we do not have the resources to wage long wars.

Figure 1.6 Wolsey's foreign policy aims

The Treaty of London, 1518

Ever ambitious, Wolsey saw his first chance to place England at the centre of European diplomacy in 1518 when he put forward the idea of a 'universal peace'. He wanted to end warfare permanently between France, England and Spain.

Under the terms of Wolsey's proposal, each state would promise to follow a non-aggressive foreign policy – which meant that neither England, France nor Spain would attack one another. If one power did go to war, they risked being attacked by the other two. The 20 leading rulers of Europe signed up to this proposal, including the pope.

The Treaty of London was a success for Henry and Wolsey.

- It brought immense prestige to Henry VIII, who came to be seen as the great European peacemaker.
- England started to be viewed as a significant power.
- It placed Henry and Wolsey at the centre of European politics – as the creators of European peace.
- It was praised across Europe as a political and diplomatic triumph.

However, the high hopes of the Treaty of London did not last. By 1521, the war between France and the Habsburg Empire had restarted. Before this, in 1519, Charles I of Spain was elected Holy Roman Emperor. He now became Charles V, Holy Roman Emperor. This event transformed European politics and made war between France and Spain inevitable, for three major reasons.

1 Francis I had hoped to gain the post of Holy Roman Emperor, but Charles was chosen instead.
2 France was now surrounded by Habsburg land.
3 As Emperor of the Holy Roman Empire, Charles had inherited a claim to the duchy of Milan, which was currently under French control.

The 'Field of the Cloth of Gold', 1520

As key figures in European diplomacy, Wolsey and Henry organised a series of conferences with Francis and Charles to prevent war. Realistically, they also wanted to see what would be offered in return for English support if a war did break out. After all, England could be a valuable ally for either side. It was well placed to invade northern France, or disrupt Spanish control of the Netherlands.

Source B

'The Field of the Cloth of Gold', painted by an unknown artist for Henry VIII, c1545.

The most spectacular of these diplomatic meetings took place between Henry and Francis in the 'Field of the Cloth of Gold', just outside Calais, in June 1520. Both men wanted to show off their prestige and so no expense was spared in a fortnight of feasting and jousting, carefully organised by Wolsey. The highpoint was an unplanned wrestling match between the two kings.

Although it was a grand occasion between two powerful monarchs, nothing of any substance was achieved.

- No decisions were made that would bring peace to Europe. This meeting merely increased suspicion in Spain that England was already taking sides.
- England's relationship with France did not improve as a result of this meeting and the two countries would be at war with each other in less than two years.

Despite this, Henry viewed the 'Field of the Cloth of Gold' as a success because it brought him immense honour and prestige. The king was exactly where he wanted to be: in the centre of European politics, meeting on equal terms with one of its superpower rulers. For Henry, appearances were everything: being seen as a great king mattered far more than ruling England effectively.

War with France, 1522–25

The Treaty of London and the 'Field of the Cloth of Gold' were the highpoints in Wolsey's foreign policy. After this, he experienced increasing difficulties and set-backs.

Francis I declared war on Charles V in April 1521. Wolsey attempted to put together a peace deal in August, but failed. With his grand hopes for 'universal peace' at an end, it now became a case of deciding which side to support. With England's political and trade interests more strongly linked with the Habsburg Empire, Henry declared war on France in May 1522.

Extend your knowledge

Wolsey and the Treaty of Bruges

Wolsey formally agreed to side with Charles V in the Treaty of Bruges in August 1521. The deal Wolsey negotiated was a good one for England. He secured a one year delay in sending an English army to France. Wolsey hoped, by this time, the conflict might be over and England would be spared the expense of war. Wolsey also welcomed the prestige gained by allying with Europe's most powerful leader.

Initially, England's contribution consisted of a minor raid on French soil led by the Earl of Surrey. In 1523, however, a triple attack on Paris was agreed between the two allies. They were to be joined by the Duke of Bourbon, a leading French nobleman who had taken up arms against Francis following a dispute over inheritance.

In August, the Duke of Suffolk began his advance on Paris with 11,000 troops. However, the promised troops from Charles never turned up, while the Duke of Bourbon failed to raise any support. Within 80 km of the capital, Suffolk was forced to retreat.

Because of these setbacks, English enthusiasm for the war declined. However, that changed when Francis and Charles fought in the Battle of Pavia, in what is now northern Italy in 1525. The outcome stunned Europe: the French army was destroyed and Francis I was taken prisoner. It was clear that Charles V had used Henry's troops to distract the French while he attacked Francis.

Henry and Wolsey immediately pressed Charles to exploit this victory by a joint invasion of the now leaderless France. Under the plan they submitted to Charles, France would be divided between the two allies and Henry would take the French crown.

Charles, however, had different ideas. He had no wish to expand Henry's power. He also released Francis after securing a promise that the humiliated French king would not seek revenge. Having been let down so obviously by their Habsburg ally, Wolsey opened negotiations with France, signing a peace treaty in 1525.

Henry's second war against France had not gone well.

- It had become obvious that Charles did not view England as an equal or valued ally.
- Charles had deserted Henry in 1523, when the Duke of Suffolk attempted to capture Paris, and had instead used English forces to distract France while he focused his efforts on the Italian peninsula (what is now known as Italy).
- Charles had not been prepared to share any of the spoils from his own success at Pavia.
- The financial cost to Henry had been high, totalling £430,000. The tax increases and forced loans had hurt Henry's popularity in England.

After three years of war, Henry had nothing to show for his efforts.

Support for France, 1525–29

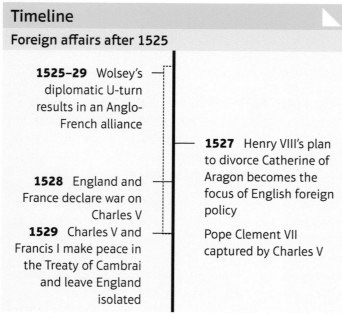

Timeline

Foreign affairs after 1525

1525–29 Wolsey's diplomatic U-turn results in an Anglo-French alliance

1527 Henry VIII's plan to divorce Catherine of Aragon becomes the focus of English foreign policy

1528 England and France declare war on Charles V

Pope Clement VII captured by Charles V

1529 Charles V and Francis I make peace in the Treaty of Cambrai and leave England isolated

The Treaty of More

Once Charles had won the Battle of Pavia, he did not repay Henry for his help. With all faith in Charles destroyed, and concern for Charles' growing power, Wolsey carried out a dramatic change in foreign policy by siding with their old enemy, France. In 1525, the Treaty of More was signed, bringing peace to the two countries. Under the treaty, Henry agreed to give up his claims to France in return for an annual payment.

The Treaty of Westminster

The following year, Wolsey helped to organise (but did not join) the **League of Cognac**. This created an alliance of France, the pope, Venice and Florence, with the aim of preventing further conquests on the Italian peninsula by Charles V. The forces of Venice and Florence then began fighting Habsburg forces, but with little success.

In 1527, Wolsey strengthened relations with France further still by signing the Treaty of Westminster. This threatened Charles with armed intervention if he did not seek to improve relations with his neighbours.

Other developments

England was now firmly committed to fighting Charles and his Habsburg Empire; but further events in 1527 caused Wolsey to question whether he had made the right decision in turning on England's former ally.

1 First, Henry began pressing for a divorce from Catherine of Aragon (see pages 29–30) and made this Wolsey's chief mission. Catherine was the aunt of Charles V.

2 Second, Habsburg troops ransacked Rome and the pope became a virtual prisoner of Charles V. This was bad news for Wolsey: the pope alone possessed the power to grant Henry's divorce, and would not do so while under the control of Catherine's nephew.

Wolsey had no control over these developments, but they significantly complicated his foreign policy. Wolsey's decision to side with France ruled out any possibility of Charles assisting Henry in seeking a divorce. Wolsey had to rely on the hope that military success by the League of Cognac would break Charles' dominance on the Italian peninsula. This was a risky strategy as Charles was very powerful.

In 1528, France and England declared war on Charles, and Francis I invaded the Italian peninsula. However, despite the declaration of war, no English troops were sent to fight. This discredited the idea that England was a serious international player.

Wolsey introduced a trade embargo* of the Netherlands, as this was part of Spain's territories. However, this was called off because of protests from English cloth workers, who needed access to the markets in Antwerp.

Most importantly, in June 1529, Charles defeated the French at the Battle of Landriano in northern Italy. As a result, Charles' power over Italy and the pope remained, and Wolsey's hopes of securing a divorce for Henry were over.

Key term

Trade embargo*
The hostile act of cutting trade links with another country.

The Treaty of Cambrai

In August 1529, following his defeat, Francis made peace with Charles in the Treaty of Cambrai. Wolsey was only informed of the peace negotiations at the last minute. England was no longer being treated as an equal by either France or the Habsburg Empire.

A summary of foreign policy under Wolsey is shown in the table opposite.

Main aims of England/Henry's policy	Successes	Failures	Mixed outcomes	Events outside of Wolsey's control
To become an internationally respected leader	Treaty of London, 1518	War against France, 1522–25	Alliance with France, 1525–29	Battle of Pavia, 1525
To achieve military victories	'Field of the Cloth of Gold', 1520	Treaty of Westminster, 1527	Treaty of More, 1525	Henry's decision to seek a divorce
To ensure England was not isolated in Europe	Treaty of Bruges, 1521	War against Charles V, 1528	League of Cognac, 1526	Capture of the pope by Charles V
		Treaty of Cambrai, 1529		

Activities

1 Make a timeline of the main foreign policy events up to 1529. For each event, say if Wolsey was following an anti-French, anti-Habsburg or neutral policy.

2 Highlight Wolsey's greatest success and greatest failure on your timeline. Explain your choices.

3 Do you think Wolsey's foreign policy was more of a success or a failure? Explain your decision.

Exam-style question, Section B

Describe **two** features of England's war with France, 1522–25. **4 marks**

Exam tip

This question is only worth four marks. You therefore need to be clear and concise in your writing. This takes practice. Also remember to give two features.

Summary

- Directing Henry's foreign policy was Wolsey's most important task. Given the relative weakness of England, this was not an easy job.
- Wolsey managed to increase English influence in Europe.
- The 'Field of the Cloth of Gold' should be viewed as one of Wolsey's greatest achievements, alongside the Treaties of London and Bruges.
- However, England was not as powerful as France or the Habsburg Empire, and struggled to compete with them.
- Wolsey's efforts to achieve military glory against France, 1522–25, achieved nothing and he was powerless to prevent Charles V from ignoring English interests.
- The French alliance of 1525–29 was a failure. It made Wolsey's task of securing Henry's divorce more difficult.

Checkpoint

Strengthen

S1 Describe what Wolsey hoped to achieve with the Treaty of London.

S2 Describe how Henry sought to portray himself as a great leader at the 'Field of the Cloth of Gold'.

S3 Explain why Wolsey decided to abandon the long-held alliance with Charles V in 1525.

Challenge

C1 'Wolsey's foreign policy failed to turn Henry into a leading player in Europe'. Write two paragraphs, one supporting and one opposing this statement.

C2 Why was it difficult for England to be a leading European power at this time?

If you are not confident answering these questions, ask your teacher for some hints.

1.4 Wolsey, Catherine, the succession and annulment

By 1527, the king was in love: but not with his wife, Catherine of Aragon. Anne Boleyn – stylish, intelligent and playful – had caught his eye. Although normally reluctant to write, passionate love letters poured out of Henry. He claimed that he had been shot by the 'dart of love'. This love affair, however, was just one part of a wider story developing in the 1520s. Focused on Henry's need for an heir, it resulted in lives being destroyed and Henry's court being transformed.

Source A

Part of a love letter from Henry VIII to Anne Boleyn, c1527.

On turning over in my mind the contents of your last letters, I have put myself into great agony, not knowing how to interpret them, whether to my disadvantage, as you show in some places, or to my advantage, as I understand them in some others, beseeching you earnestly to let me know expressly your whole mind as to the love between us two. It is absolutely necessary for me to obtain this answer, having been for above a whole year stricken with the dart of love.

Catherine of Aragon and the succession

For two decades, Henry had been, in many ways, a caring and affectionate husband, in love with his wife. In return, Catherine of Aragon had been a loyal wife, supporting him when he needed her.

Henry first met Catherine when he was a young prince and she was betrothed to his older brother, Arthur. As she was the princess of Spain, this was a political marriage to join the two nations in an alliance. They married in November 1501, but Arthur died unexpectedly the following April. It was decreed by the pope that the marriage had not been consummated*.

This was important: it meant Catherine could be married to Prince Henry instead, and the Anglo–Spanish alliance maintained.

There was genuine affection between the royal couple, and Catherine became everything a 16th-century queen should be. Deeply religious, educated and regal, she became widely respected among the English people for her charitable work. She also defended Henry's interests. In 1513, Henry appointed her as his regent* while he led an invasion of France.

Extend your knowledge

The Battle of Flodden, 1513
When the Scottish king, James IV, took advantage of Henry's absence in France by marching south to invade England, Catherine sent an army to defeat him in the Battle of Flodden. James IV was killed, and Catherine sent his bloodied shirt to Henry in France as a gift.

Catherine had many difficult pregnancies. Primary sources confirm she was pregnant six times, with only one baby, Mary, surviving. The emotional and physical toll on the queen must have been terrible. By 1524, Henry had stopped sleeping with Catherine. Aged 39, her chances of becoming pregnant again were low. Unfortunately for Catherine, she had failed to provide Henry with the one thing he needed: a surviving son.

Key terms

Consummated*
Confirming a marriage by having sex: a marriage was not considered valid until then.

Regent*
A person who governs the kingdom in the king's absence.

Henry's reasons for seeking an annulment

Catherine's unhappy history of childbirth was not just a personal tragedy. It was also a political problem and led to Henry seeking the annulment* of their marriage in 1527. Henry believed that he needed a healthy male heir in order to guarantee the future of the Tudor dynasty.

Having only a female heir might encourage others with a claim to the throne – both at home and abroad – to challenge for the throne.

Key term

Annulment*

A legal term declaring that a marriage was never valid, and therefore never existed. An annulment could only be granted by the pope.

Extend your knowledge

Henry Fitzroy (1519–36)
In his search for a male heir, Henry started to take steps to ensure his illegitimate son, Henry Fitzroy, would succeed him. Henry Fitzroy was the son of Henry and his mistress, Bessie Blount. In 1525, Fitzroy was made Duke of Richmond (see also page 48).

Henry also started to view Catherine's failure to produce a son as a sign of God's displeasure. The king reasoned that there could be no physical reason for a lack of healthy children, as he was strong and healthy and had produced a healthy son with his mistress. Instead, God must be punishing him because He disapproved of Henry's marriage to his brother's widow. Henry found support for this in the Bible (see Source B).

Source B

An extract from Leviticus, a book in the Bible, supporting Henry's case for a divorce.

If a man shall take his brother's wife it is an impurity: ... they shall be childless.

There was also a more personal reason for seeking an annulment. Henry was deeply in love with Anne Boleyn, who was everything Catherine was not. The queen was in her forties and had lost her looks. As early as 1519, Francis I had commented on Henry's 'old deformed wife'. Anne, in contrast, was young and beautiful.

Source C

Anne Boleyn, c1533–36, by an unknown artist. Edward Hall, a Tudor MP, described her as having a long neck, wide mouth and 'eyes which were black and beautiful'. The portrait also shows her wearing her famous 'B' pendant.

Henry already knew Anne's family. Anne was the daughter of Sir Thomas Boleyn, a courtier and minister, and was the niece of the Duke of Norfolk, who was becoming a key adviser to the king.

Anne refused the king's initial advances, letting it be known that she would only sleep with him when they were married. This strategy worked and made the king all the more determined to secure an annulment.

Henry's attempts to gain an annulment

The task of getting the annulment of Henry's marriage to Catherine fell to Wolsey in 1527. Although this required the approval of the pope, Wolsey assured Henry that this could be easily achieved. As cardinal and Papal Legate, as well as an internationally respected statesman, Wolsey had influence in Rome. He also assumed the pope would want to help Henry, who was his ally.

However, it soon became clear that Rome was not going to co-operate. As seen previously, Charles V was the nephew of Catherine, and his victory over the French at Pavia in 1525 left him dominating Rome. For a short time in 1527, he even imprisoned the pope. This caused problems for Wolsey. For the pope, the risk of upsetting Charles V by granting the annulment was too great. At the same time, the pope did not want to lose the support of his English ally. The result was a papal policy that delayed making a final decision for as long as possible.

With pressure mounting from Henry, Anne Boleyn and her supporters, Wolsey tried a range of strategies, hoping one would pay off.

First, Wolsey tried to find evidence in the Bible to support an annulment. Henry had only been allowed to marry Catherine as a result of a special dispensation (permission) from the pope. Based on Henry's interpretation of Leviticus, a book of the Bible, it was argued that the dispensation should never have been granted because it broke God's law. However, this approach ran into three main problems.

1   Supporters of Catherine pointed to a passage from Deuteronomy, another book of the Bible (Source D), which suggested that a man could marry his brother's widow and have children with her. Despite a huge theological debate, there was no clear answer to who was right or wrong.

2   Henry's Leviticus argument only worked if Catherine and Arthur had been 'properly married'. She consistently denied that the marriage had been consummated. The only evidence Wolsey had that it had been consummated was court gossip, and Arthur's statement after their wedding night that he had spent the night in the 'midst of Spain'.

3   It would be embarrassing for the pope to admit the original dispensation was a mistake.

Source D

An extract from Deuteronomy, a book of the Bible, used to undermine Henry's case for divorce.

When brethren dwell together, and one of them dieth without children, the wife of the deceased shall not marry to another; but his brother shall take her, and raise up seed [have children] for his brother.

Activity ?

In small groups, study the Leviticus and Deuteronomy quotes in Sources B and D. One side can argue their meaning from the point-of-view of Henry VIII, and the other from Catherine of Aragon's viewpoint.

Another approach from Wolsey focused on challenging the pope's original decision to allow Henry and Catherine to marry on technical grounds. By arguing that it was incorrectly worded, it would make the marriage between Henry and Catherine invalid. This approach had the advantage of giving Rome a non-controversial reason for annulling the marriage. However, Catherine's supporters found a correctly worded Spanish version of the decision – Wolsey could no longer use it as an argument for the annulment.

Meanwhile, huge pressure was placed on Catherine to renounce her marriage and become a nun. This would automatically terminate the marriage and so avoid the need for the pope's approval. In one message sent to Catherine, the king warned her that, if an attempt was made on his life, she would be blamed for it. The message accused her of hating the king and becoming too friendly with the public by nodding, smiling and waving to them. Furthermore, he would no longer see their daughter, Princess Mary. It was a cruel letter designed to force her into becoming a nun, but it did not work.

Wolsey's final attempt to annul the marriage was focused on persuading Rome to allow the case to be decided in England. As Papal Legate, the decision would then fall to Wolsey, who would do as the king wished. Long discussions followed as the precise arrangements were worked out. Eventually, a compromise was reached in April 1528. Cardinal Campeggio and Cardinal Wolsey would rule on behalf of the pope in England. Henry believed nothing else would now get in his way.

However promising, this approach also failed.

Interpretation 1

Taken from Lucy Wooding's *Henry VIII* (2009), this interpretation highlights a crucial point about the relationship between Henry and Wolsey, and how that affected Wolsey's downfall.

In the summer of 1529, it was clear that Henry had suffered a major defeat, and that a new approach was needed. New blood, it seemed, was also wanted. The first casualty of the debacle at Blackfriars was Wolsey. Formerly adept at bringing the king everything he wanted, particularly when it came to ecclesiastical [Church] and diplomatic affairs, Wolsey had spectacularly failed to bring Henry the thing he wanted more than anything else. This underlines a crucial point about Wolsey's place in Henry's life: he did not dominate the king, as some have suggested; he served him, and when he ceased to serve him to Henry's satisfaction, he fell from power.

Why did the case for the annulment fail?

- Cardinal Campeggio had been given instructions by the pope not to reach a final verdict.
- Campeggio's delaying tactics made Henry frustrated. The Cardinal only arrived in England in October 1528 – though this was partly due to illness.
- When the case finally opened in Blackfriars court in June 1529, Campeggio insisted on doing everything by the book.
- In July 1529, Campeggio broke up the court for the summer without a final decision being reached.

Unfortunately for Henry and Wolsey, Campeggio was near the end of his life and could not be pressured into making a decision. Instead, Henry's anger was taken out on Wolsey. The fact that this had been another dead-end became clear when the pope decided, at the end of the summer of 1529, that the matter had to be heard in Rome after all.

Opposition to the annulment

The annulment hearing was held at Blackfriars court. During the hearing, Catherine of Aragon was called to speak. She ignored the officials and made her way over to her husband. She knelt before him and delivered her plea not to cast her aside. This was one example of the total opposition Catherine had to the idea of a divorce.

Catherine could stand up to Henry because she had powerful supporters, including **John Fisher**, the highly respected Bishop of Rochester, and **Thomas More**, adviser to the king. Public support for the queen was also strong. And she had the backing of Europe's most powerful man, Charles V, her nephew.

Because of Catherine's family connection with Charles, the pope was simply not in a position to support an annulment.

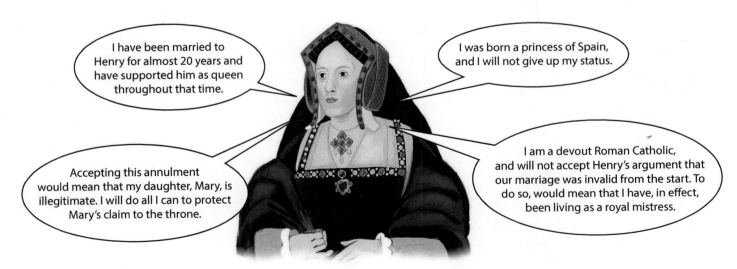

Figure 1.7 Catherine of Aragon's opposition to the annulment.

Reasons for Wolsey's fall

Wolsey's end came quickly. When Campeggio suspended work on the divorce case in July 1529, it was clear that the chief minister's divorce strategy had failed. In October, Henry punished Wolsey by stripping him of most of his powers and possessions, and exiling him to York. In November 1530, Wolsey was summoned to London for trial on charges of *praemunire**. His health broken, Wolsey died on the journey southwards and so was spared the fate of almost certain execution. His last words expressed regret that he had served his king better than his God.

Henry's faith in Wolsey was undermined by three high profile failures.

1   His failure with the Amicable Grant.
2   His failure to secure the annulment for Henry.
3   His failure to build an alliance against Charles V.

The influence of the Boleyn family

Wolsey's downfall was also caused by the influence of the Boleyn family. The Eltham Ordinances highlighted

> ### Key term
>
> *Praemunire**
> Treason by a member of the clergy as a result of working in the interests of the pope, not the king.

how Wolsey sought to prevent rivals from gaining close access to the king. Up until 1527, he was largely successful. As the relationship between Henry and Anne developed, Wolsey was unable to prevent a powerful new group in court developing around Anne, led by her father Thomas Boleyn and her brother, George.

The Boleyns argued that Wolsey was deliberately trying to disrupt the divorce proceedings. They said he favoured Catherine and believed the king would tire of Anne. As each effort failed, so their attacks on the chief minister increased. Anne in particular grew to hate Wolsey. Many other nobles with grudges against Wolsey eagerly sided with them. With the final failure of proceedings in summer 1529, the Boleyns helped persuade Henry that Wolsey had to go.

Summary

- Henry's need for a son, his worries about the validity of his marriage in the eyes of God, and his love for Anne Boleyn, all contributed to the king's decision to seek an annulment.
- Wolsey was charged with this task and pursued a wide variety of strategies. The most hopeful was having the case heard in England – but Cardinal Campeggio proved unwilling to give the verdict Henry wanted.
- Wolsey failed to secure an annulment because he could not overcome the queen's determined opposition, and because the pope was dominated by Catherine's nephew and supporter, Charles V.
- Wolsey's failure led to his downfall, as the king lost confidence in him, encouraged by the powerful Boleyn faction. He was charged with *praemunire*, but did not live to face trial.

Checkpoint

Strengthen

S1 Summarise, in no more than 200 words, the four main strategies used by Wolsey to obtain an annulment.

S2 Describe why the annulment hearing at Blackfriars court did not go according to Wolsey's plan.

Challenge

C1 Which reason do you think was most important in encouraging Henry to seek an annulment – his need for a male heir, his moral concerns over his marriage, or his love for Anne Boleyn?

C2 Was Henry right to blame Wolsey for the failure to obtain an annulment?

If you are not confident about any of these questions, discuss the answers with other students and record your conclusions.

Recap: Henry VIII and Wolsey, 1509–29

Recall quiz

1 What was the size of England's population when Henry became king in 1509?

2 Why was a papal dispensation needed before Henry VIII could marry Catherine of Aragon?

3 List the key parts of government at the time of Henry VIII.

4 Name the important government position granted to Wolsey in 1515.

5 How much money did Wolsey raise through the subsidy up to 1529?

6 Describe the Eltham Ordinances.

7 Name the two most powerful leaders in Europe that Wolsey had to deal with, and the countries they ruled over.

8 Why was 1525 a significant year in Wolsey's foreign policy?

9 Give two reasons why Henry VIII became convinced that his marriage to Catherine was not supported by God.

10 What name is given to the powerful group in Henry's court that opposed Wolsey?

Exam-style question, Section B

'Wolsey's failure to gain an annulment for Henry was the main reason why he fell from power in 1529'.

How far do you agree? Explain your answer. You may use the following in your answer:

- The treaty with France
- The Boleyn faction.

You **must** also use information of your own. **16 marks**

Activities

1 Imagine that you have been placed in charge of teaching a pupil in the year below about Henry VIII. For each of the following topics, decide what four key points you would want them to learn.

　a England in 1509

　b Henry's coronation

　c Henry's marriage to Catherine of Aragon

　d The rise of Thomas Wolsey

　e Wolsey's economic policies

　f Wolsey's foreign policy

2 Wolsey became the second most important person in England. Identify specific factors behind Wolsey's rise to power. Historians normally focus on his **intelligence**, **charm**, **capacity for hard work**, **exceptional ability** and **luck**. Provide at least one piece of specific evidence to support each factor. Rank them in order of importance.

Exam tip

To do well in this question, identify three or four reasons to explain why Wolsey fell from power. Ensure you have accurate and relevant historical knowledge to expand upon each of your key points and decide which reasons were the most important.

Writing historically: managing sentences

Successful historical writing is clearly expressed, using carefully managed sentence structures.

Learning outcomes

By the end of this lesson, you will understand how to:

- select and use single clause and multiple clause sentences.

Definitions

Clause: a group of words or unit of meaning that contains a verb and can form part or all of a sentence, e.g. 'Thomas Wolsey was Henry VIII's chief minister'.

Single clause sentence: a sentence containing just one clause, e.g. 'Thomas Wolsey was Henry VIII's chief minister'.

Multiple clause sentence: a sentence containing two or more clauses, often linked with a conjunction, e.g. 'Thomas Wolsey was Henry VIII's chief minister and he dominated government for 15 years'.

Co-ordinating conjunction: a word used to link two clauses of equal importance within a sentence, e.g. 'and', 'but', 'so', 'or', etc.

How can I structure my sentences clearly?

When you are explaining and exploring complex events and ideas, you can end up writing very long sentences. These can make your writing difficult for the reader to follow.

Look at the extract below from a response to this exam-style question:

> Describe **two** features of the Field of the Cloth of Gold. **(4 marks)**

> *The Field of the Cloth of Gold, organised by Cardinal Wolsey, was a high level meeting between Henry VIII and Francis I, the King of France, both young, ambitious rulers who were keen to impress each other, in 1520.*

1. The writer of the response above has linked every piece of information in his answer into one, very long sentence.

How many different pieces of information has the writer included in this answer? Rewrite each piece of information as a **single clause sentence**. For example:

> *The Field of the Cloth of Gold was organised by Cardinal Wolsey.*

2. Look again at your answer to Question 1. Which of the single clause sentences would you link together? Rewrite the response twice, experimenting with linking different sentences together using co-ordinating **conjunctions** such as 'and', 'but' or 'so'. Remember: you are aiming to make your writing as clear and precise as possible.

3. Now write a paragraph in response to the exam-style question below, using only single clause sentences to state each different piece of information.

> Describe **two** features of England's war with France, 1522–25. **(4 marks)**

4. Now rewrite your response to Question 3. Experiment with linking different sentences together using co-ordination conjunctions such as 'and', 'but' or 'so'. Remember: you are aiming to make your writing as clear and precise as possible.

How can I use conjunctions to link my ideas?

There are several types of **multiple clause sentence** structures that you can use to link your ideas.

If you want to balance or contrast two ideas of equal importance within a sentence, you can use co-ordinating conjunctions to link them.

Look at the extract below from a response to this exam-style question:

> Explain why Henry VIII wanted to annul his marriage to Catherine of Aragon in 1527. **(12 marks)**

> *Nature doomed their marriage. Catherine miscarried five times and had only a daughter and in 1527 was middle-aged. This not only made her unlikely to provide another male heir in the future but also made Henry doubt the legitimacy of their marriage. In the end he wanted an annulment not through conscience but because he feared for his succession and he had fallen for another woman, Anne Boleyn.*

These co-ordinating conjunctions link equally important actions that happened at the same time.

These paired co-ordinating conjunctions contrast two possible causes.

These paired co-ordinating conjunctions link and balance two equally important ideas.

5. How else could the writer of the response above have linked, balanced or contrasted these ideas? Experiment with rewriting the response, using different sentence structures, and different ways of linking ideas within them using co-ordinating conjunctions.

Did you notice?

The first sentence in the response above is a single clause sentence, containing one verb:

> *Nature doomed their marriage.*

6. Why do you think the writer chose to give this point additional emphasis by structuring it as a short, single clause sentence? Write a sentence or two explaining your ideas.

Improving an answer

7. Now look at the final paragraph below of the response to the exam-style question above.

> *Henry's rival, Francis I, called Catherine Henry's 'old deformed wife'. Anne Boleyn was young and beautiful. Anne resisted Henry's advances. Anne insisted Henry must first make her his wife. Henry was in love. He was determined to win Anne. She promised him everything he wanted.*

Rewrite this paragraph, choosing some conjunctions from the **Co-ordinating Conjunction Bank** below to link, balance or contrast the writer's ideas.

Co-ordinating Conjunction Bank	
and	not only... but
but	also...
or	either... or
so	neither... nor
	both... and

02 | Henry VIII and Cromwell, 1529–40

Henry VIII was in his mid-forties by the end of the 1520s. The gentle, open and handsome man from the start of his reign was now gone.

Henry wanted huge religious and government reforms. His search for a son was equally determined, and had already led to the banishment of one wife. By 1536, he had executed another. However, not everything was under the king's control. Fifteen thirty seven saw Henry suffer the heartache of losing his third, and much loved, wife in childbirth.

Another significant power in England at this time was a Putney 'ruffian' called Thomas Cromwell. Just like Wolsey, he had risen from nothing to become Henry's right-hand man. Many people see Cromwell as a shadowy schemer who used plotting and torture to get ahead in the world; though some see him as the king's loyal servant, prepared to take the difficult decisions needed by his master.

However he is remembered, Cromwell made many bitter enemies. In 1540, these enemies saw their moment to bring him down. Cromwell's end was quick and shows clearly the brutal side of Henry's England.

Learning outcomes

When you have finished studying this chapter, you will:

- understand how Thomas Cromwell rose to become Henry's chief minister
- understand the key role Cromwell played in bringing about Henry VIII's divorce from Catherine of Aragon
- understand the reasons behind the fall of Anne Boleyn, as well as the impact of Henry's short marriage to Jane Seymour
- know how Cromwell reformed both government and finance
- understand why Cromwell fell from power in 1540.

Learning outcomes

- Know about Cromwell's early life, and his service with both Wolsey and Henry VIII.
- Understand how Cromwell secured Henry's annulment.

Cromwell's early life

Fourteen eighty five saw the birth of a healthy boy, called Thomas, to Katherine and Walter Cromwell of Putney. For a man who would one day become the most powerful man in England (apart from the king) the start of Thomas' life held no glamour and little promise.

Putney was a bustling, but far from wealthy, Thames-side town near London. Thomas Cromwell's father was a blacksmith, a cloth worker and an ale-house keeper. He was also a scoundrel. Walter got into fights, watered down the beer in his inn and let his cattle graze too freely on public land.

The relationship between father and son was troubled. Cromwell inherited his father's unruly streak. He later told the Archbishop of Canterbury, Thomas Cranmer, that he had been a 'ruffian… in his young days'. It is unlikely that Cromwell went to school. He was also often at the receiving end of his father's violent temper.

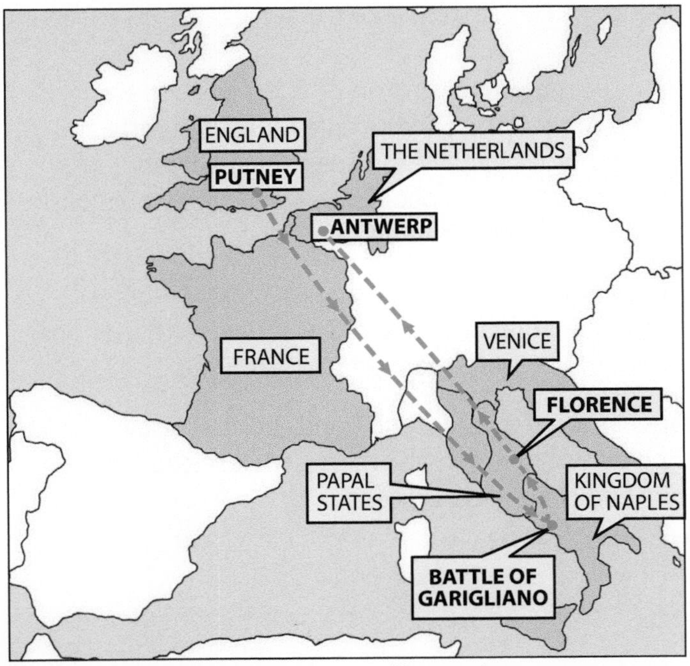

Figure 2.1 A map showing Cromwell's travels as a young man.

In 1503, Cromwell, either because of a fight with his father or trouble with the law, decided to leave England. In an age when very few people left their own town, this was very brave.

With a young man's spirit for adventure, he joined the French army and fought against the Spanish in the Battle of Garigliano, in the Italian peninsula, in December 1503. After a crushing defeat, Cromwell deserted the French army and moved to Florence. He used his hard work, charm and sharp mind to rise up in the household of Francesco Frescobaldi, a leading merchant banker. Cromwell was living in the city at the heart of the Renaissance. This gave him a lifelong love for art, literature and music.

Cromwell later described himself as 'a great traveller in this world', and he believed this set him apart from others. After Florence, Cromwell became a cloth merchant in Antwerp (in Belgium). It was the perfect environment for him to develop his trading knowledge and make important business contacts.

In around 1514, Cromwell returned to England, married Elizabeth Wyckes (who came from a very wealthy family), and established himself as a London merchant. Although he lacked any formal legal training, Cromwell also developed a thriving legal practice. He had learned enough about law in Europe to gain business and a reputation. Cromwell's years in Europe had, therefore, changed the boy into a man. He had been transformed from a Putney 'ruffian' to a cultured and successful man of business.

Cromwell's service to Wolsey

Cromwell was ambitious. In addition to running his merchant and legal businesses, he also entered Thomas Wolsey's household soon after returning to England. Working for the *Alter Rex* brought with it a lot of respect, and opportunities for further advancement.

Extend your knowledge

Cromwell helps Wolsey

In the mid-1520s, Cromwell organised the closure of 30 small monasteries to fund Wolsey's two pet projects: the setting up of Cardinal College in Oxford, and King's School in Ipswich. Closing these monasteries was controversial, and legally it was an extraordinarily complex task.

By 1519, Cromwell was a member of Wolsey's Council. By 1529, he was his most trusted adviser. This should not be surprising. While Wolsey was 15 years his senior, the two men had a lot in common. They were both self-made men, who had risen from humble origins through intelligence, and hard work.

Over the course of the 1520s, Cromwell started to develop a name for himself in Henry's court.

- He took on increasingly high profile legal cases, many being heard in the Star Chamber.
- Wolsey frequently sent Cromwell to deliver news to the king.
- In 1523, Cromwell became a Member of Parliament (MP) for the first time.

Cromwell's personality

When you first look at Source A, you might think Cromwell was a grumpy man, surrounded by his work. The portrait certainly does him no favours. He has a double chin, small eyes, a large nose and dull clothes. However, if you look more closely, aspects of Cromwell's character become clearer. His lips are pressed together in concentration. His eyes are staring off into the distance and his eyebrows are raised slightly. It is as though Cromwell is deep in thought, pondering a great matter of state before coming up with the necessary solution.

The artist has captured Cromwell's focus, intelligence and determination. He has also given an insight into a man who could keep his emotions in check. As will be seen later in this chapter, Cromwell was prepared to make difficult decisions – which meant even sending people to die. Cromwell's clothes reflect his distaste for showiness. Not that he had much choice – in Henry's court, there were strict laws governing dress. For example, only the king could wear purple. Cromwell's low birth meant he would not be allowed to wear rich colours.

Cromwell was more than the man shown in Source A. He was also warm and charming. He enjoyed conversation and people found him witty and interesting. According to Eustace Chapuys, the Spanish ambassador of Charles V, he used his personality to win people over, and they would often end up telling him far more than they intended.

In his personal life, Cromwell was a loving husband and father – but, tragically, his wife and two daughters, Anne and Grace, died in the summer of 1528 from sweating sickness. His one son, Gregory, survived.

Cromwell was also noted as a caring and loyal friend, which Wolsey discovered near the end of his life. When all others had deserted him, Cromwell defended him and remained his friend.

Source A

Thomas Cromwell, painted by Hans Holbein, 1532. The letter on top of the pile is inscribed 'To Master Cromwell, trusty and well-beloved master of our jewel house'.

Activity ?

Create a timeline showing the events of Cromwell's early life

Serving Henry VIII

Thomas Wolsey's dramatic fall from power in the autumn of 1529 changed everything for Thomas Cromwell. In a rare display of emotion, Cromwell cried when he heard the news of his master's death. He may have also been thinking of his own future – which also looked bleak.

- Cromwell's hopes of building a dazzling career in court now seemed at an end. Without Wolsey, he had no formal position in Henry's government.
- As Wolsey's most senior adviser, Cromwell was also in a dangerous position. The bitter attacks being made against his master could easily include him, too.

Election as an MP

However, Cromwell did not believe in self-pity or disloyalty. Many members of Wolsey's household distanced themselves from the cardinal.

Cromwell, however, did the opposite. He successfully became the MP for Taunton in 1529 and used this position to speak in Wolsey's defence. He also tried to defend Wolsey in court, even gaining audiences with the king himself.

Membership of the Royal Council

While ultimately unsuccessful in saving his master, Cromwell impressed Henry with his loyalty, as well as the skill he had shown in managing Wolsey's legal affairs after his death. This included sorting out what happened to his many properties and huge staff. The king was in need of talented men. In 1531, Cromwell was appointed to the Royal Council, placing him in Henry's circle of trusted advisers. Cromwell realised that helping Henry to divorce Catherine of Aragon would be a sure way of gaining further promotion.

Securing Henry's annulment

Following Wolsey's fall in 1529, Henry's campaign to secure an annulment from Catherine of Aragon achieved little. He asked leading nobles, including the Duke of Norfolk and the Duke of Suffolk, as well as Anne Boleyn's own father (made Earl of Wiltshire in 1529) to look at the case. However, they lacked the necessary talent and skill to come up with a winning strategy to legally gain the divorce.

In addition to this, Thomas More was Henry's new Lord Chancellor. Sympathetic to Catherine of Aragon and a devout Catholic, More opposed the divorce. In fact, his differences with Henry became so great that he retired in 1532, telling people he was too ill to continue as Lord Chancellor.

Cromwell's plan to secure Henry's annulment

In 1531, Cromwell started working on the case for Henry. He realised that the pope would never decide in Henry's favour, and so there was little point continuing to argue the case in Rome. An ideas man, Cromwell supplied the solution to Henry's problem.

- The power to grant an annulment should be removed from the pope and given to Henry instead.
- To provide the legal basis for this, parliament could be used to pass a law transferring the power.

While it may appear a logical, and even simple, solution, what Cromwell was proposing was ground-breaking.

- Cromwell was directly challenging the pope, who was the established leader of the Christian Church. The pope had always ruled on matters of religion in England before this.
- Cromwell was dramatically expanding the role of parliament. Up until this point, it had mainly been used to grant new taxes. Now it would be used to influence the highest laws in the kingdom.

By January 1533, Anne Boleyn was pregnant, so Henry needed a divorce more than ever. He had to marry Anne Boleyn before she gave birth for the child to be his legitimate heir.

| Cromwell seeks his fortune | Cromwell the merchant | Cromwell the family man | Cromwell and Wolsey | Cromwell in parliament | Cromwell and Henry |

Figure 2.2 Thomas Cromwell: from Putney ruffian to chief minister.

On 25 January, the new Archbishop of Canterbury, Thomas Cranmer, performed a secret marriage ceremony for the couple. This, however, was not legal. In the eyes of the Catholic Church, Henry was still married to Catherine of Aragon. Unless this changed, the baby Anne was carrying would be illegitimate.

In March 1533, the **Act in Restraint of Appeals** was passed. This Act would go on to become the basis of granting Henry's divorce.

Source B

The introduction to the Act in Restraint of Appeals, 1533.

... [I]t is manifestly declared and expressed that this realm of England is an empire, and so hath been accepted in this world, governed by one Supreme Head and King...

The Act stated that England was 'an empire' and so was not subject to any form of foreign rule – which included the pope. Furthermore, the king was the 'Supreme Head' of England and so ruled over every aspect of his kingdom. This statement meant that all powers held by the pope now belonged to Henry. He was now Supreme Head of the Church in England and he, rather than the pope in Rome, had the right to grant annulments.

A divorce hearing began in May 1533, headed by Archbishop Cranmer. Catherine refused to recognise the legitimacy of the court and did not attend. On 23 May, the court announced that:

- the original papal dispensation had been invalid
- Henry and Catherine had never been legally married
- Henry's secret marriage to Anne was therefore legal because he was a bachelor at the time.

After six years, Henry had finally got his wish. A week after the hearing, great celebrations were held to mark Anne Boleyn's coronation as queen. Spread over four days, the celebrations saw Anne travel from Greenwich Palace to the Tower of London. She was accompanied by over 300 boats, hung with banners and flags. Anne was triumphantly carried through London under a canopy of gold cloth before she was crowned queen.

However, there was an anti-climax to these celebrations. In September, Anne Boleyn gave birth to a girl – Elizabeth Tudor. Henry was disappointed. He had not gained the son he wanted.

Extend your knowledge

The new Queen of England

Anne Boleyn's coronation was designed to be extravagant. Henry wanted his subjects and the invited foreign guests to share his joy at his new marriage. He also wanted them to be left in no doubt that Anne was now Queen of England. He was aware that the marriage was very controversial, and that Catherine of Aragon continued to be held in high regard by many. Henry hoped the four-day celebration would start winning people over to his new queen.

Henry's chief minister

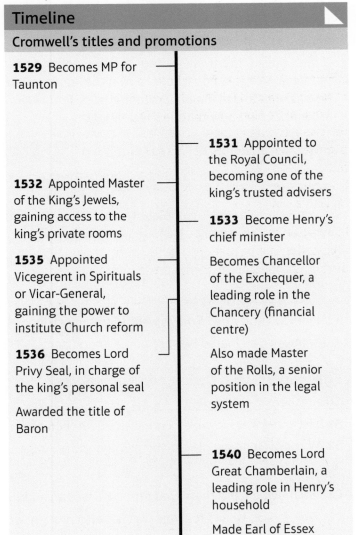

Timeline

Cromwell's titles and promotions

1529 Becomes MP for Taunton

1531 Appointed to the Royal Council, becoming one of the king's trusted advisers

1532 Appointed Master of the King's Jewels, gaining access to the king's private rooms

1533 Become Henry's chief minister

Becomes Chancellor of the Exchequer, a leading role in the Chancery (financial centre)

1535 Appointed Vicegerent in Spirituals or Vicar-General, gaining the power to institute Church reform

Also made Master of the Rolls, a senior position in the legal system

1536 Becomes Lord Privy Seal, in charge of the king's personal seal

Awarded the title of Baron

1540 Becomes Lord Great Chamberlain, a leading role in Henry's household

Made Earl of Essex

Securing Henry's divorce from Catherine of Aragon was Cromwell's big break. From 1533 until his death in 1540, he acted as Henry's chief minister. He was the man who Henry went to for advice. Cromwell's task was to implement the royal will – which meant giving Henry everything he wanted.

As the timeline shows, he was rewarded with many titles and offices, and these gave Cromwell a leading say in the kingdom's legal, religious and financial affairs. However, while certainly becoming powerful and rich, Cromwell was no *Alter Rex* like his predecessor, Wolsey.

- He was not given as much freedom as Wolsey to decide on policy. Henry was no longer a young man mainly interested in pleasure. Instead, Henry had taken a more direct role in government and so looked to his chief minister to carry out his instructions quickly and efficiently.

- Unlike Wolsey, Cromwell was not extravagant and did not develop a vast household to rival the king's. When he was not entertaining important guests, Cromwell's account books show that he lived simply.

- Henry was careful not to make Cromwell too powerful. Cromwell was not given as many titles and promotions as Wolsey had. For example, Cromwell was never formally made head of the Royal Council with the title Lord Chancellor.

Like his former master, however, Cromwell's position depended on his ability to do what the king asked by thinking through problems and coming up with solutions.

Exam-style question, Section B

Explain why Cromwell rose to become Henry's chief minister. You may use the following in your answer:

- Cromwell's work with Wolsey
- the annulment.

You **must** also use information of your own. **12 marks**

Exam tip

To gain high marks, remember to provide accurate and precisely selected information to back up your points.

Summary

- Cromwell was born into humble origins. His rise to power was helped by travels in Europe and his work for Wolsey.
- Cromwell gained the complete trust of Henry VIII by securing his divorce from Catherine of Aragon.
- Cromwell's solution was radical and involved transferring the powers held by Rome to the king.
- Parliament was used to make this happen by passing the Act in Restraint of Appeals.
- The power to grant annulments was now with the Crown and not Rome. A new divorce court was established which granted Henry's annulment on 23 May 1533.
- Henry VIII and Anne Boleyn were secretly married in January 1533. She was crowned queen on 1 June 1533.
- Cromwell dominated Henry's government from 1533 to 1540, acting as his chief minister.

Checkpoint

Strengthen

S1 List three ways in which Cromwell's European travels aided his rise to power.

S2 Why did Henry want to divorce Catherine of Aragon?

Challenge

C1 What evidence is there that Cromwell was an ambitious man? Find at least five points.

C2 Why do you think Cromwell was not also brought down when Wolsey fell from power?

C3 Why do you think Cromwell's solution for securing a divorce had not been attempted by Wolsey?

How confident do you feel about your answers to these questions? Form a group with other students, discuss the answers and then record your conclusions. Your teacher can give you some hints.

2.2 Cromwell and the king's marriages

Learning outcomes

- Understand the reasons for the fall of Anne Boleyn.
- Understand the importance of the Seymours and Cromwell in the fall of Anne Boleyn.

Reasons for the fall of Anne Boleyn

On 7 January 1536, Catherine of Aragon died. Henry VIII and Anne Boleyn did nothing to hide their joy. Henry dressed in yellow, except for a white feather in his bonnet, and went to mass accompanied by trumpets. Anne, now pregnant again, also wore yellow. While this was the colour of official mourning in Spain, it most certainly was not in England. Henry and Anne's conduct reflected the new style of their court. Whereas Catherine of Aragon had ruled over a modest and serious court, Anne encouraged music, dancing and entertainment on a huge scale. In this atmosphere, scandal and gossip were common.

Henry and Anne's happiness was not to last. Later that month, Henry fell from his horse while jousting and was unconscious for two hours. Onlookers feared the worst – they thought the king would die. Although Henry recovered, his leg suffered permanent damage and the great athlete was never to joust again.

Then, possibly on 29 January, the day of Catherine's funeral, Anne miscarried. She later claimed it was brought on by the shock of Henry's accident. Her husband offered no sympathy. Within four months of this trauma, Anne found herself being accused of adultery* with five men, including her own brother. Taken to the Tower of London, she was sentenced to death by either beheading or burning.

What had happened? Henry had pursued Anne for six years and yet ended the relationship with terrifying swiftness. Why had his feelings changed so quickly?

Key term

Adultery*

When a married person has sexual relations with someone other than their husband or wife.

Henry's desire for a son

In the end, Anne was no different to Catherine of Aragon. She had failed to provide Henry with the one thing he so desperately wanted – a son.

Anne's first child, born in September 1533, was a girl. Although Henry was disappointed, the fact that his wife had conceived so quickly and given birth without complications seemed a good sign for the future. However, it is likely that Anne suffered a miscarriage in 1534. A further miscarriage in 1536 then proved fatal for the royal marriage. By this point, Henry needed a male heir more than ever.

Why was Henry so desperate for a male heir?

- In 1536, Henry turned 45. In Tudor times, this was the beginning of old age.
- The fall from his horse had made Henry scared he could die without having a son.
- The security of his kingdom was in danger. As a result of his break with Rome, the pope had drawn up, but not yet issued, a papal bull* stating that England would be given to anyone who could take it. This put him under threat from France and Spain.

Key term

Papal bull*

A very important document issued by the pope, giving his view or instructions on a particular matter. All Catholics, including kings, were expected to follow what was said in a papal bull.

As he had done with his marriage before, Henry once again reasoned that God disapproved of his marriage and so was refusing to provide him with a son. Evidence that Henry's feelings had changed can be seen in Henry's visit to Anne shortly after hearing the news of her miscarriage. According to the Spanish ambassador, Chapuys, he said very little, except 'I see that God will not give me male children'.

Extend your knowledge

Anne's miscarriage
Some historians have argued that Anne gave birth to a deformed baby in 1536. If so, this would have provided Henry with further evidence of God's displeasure. It would also have raised suspicion that Anne was a witch. However, there is no real evidence to support this theory. It was probably a lie.

By 1536, Henry was also growing disappointed with his wife for other reasons. Her quick, sharp mind and assertive personality had once been attractive to him. These qualities had been refreshingly different and contrasted well with the obedient attitude of Catherine of Aragon. Now, Henry started to find Anne irritating.

The appearance of the sweet and homely Jane Seymour convinced Henry even more that he needed to get rid of Anne. At some point in 1536, Henry moved beyond merely wanting to make Jane his mistress. Instead, he wanted her as his wife.

Extend your knowledge

The rise of Jane Seymour
The rise of Jane Seymour was no accident. She was helped by a conservative group in court who wanted to see Anne Boleyn fall. Powerful individuals like the Duke of Norfolk (Anne's own uncle) grew to dislike Anne Boleyn for what they saw as her meddling in the political and religious affairs of England.

Anne's suspected adultery

By mid-1536, the atmosphere in Henry's court was poisonous. Although the origin is not clear, a rumour reached the king that his wife was being unfaithful. Perhaps if Anne had been able to provide Henry with a son, this would have been dismissed as just court gossip. Instead, Henry decided to take it seriously. On 24 April, he asked Cromwell to investigate.

On 30 April, Mark Smeaton, a court musician, was arrested, taken to Cromwell's house and (probably) tortured. He confessed to having an affair with the queen. Further arrests soon followed until a case had been built up. The queen was charged with five cases of adultery and treason (betraying the king) against the king.

Jane Seymour

Source A

A portrait of Jane Seymour, painted by Hans Holbein.

Arrests made for adultery and treason

1   Mark Smeaton, aged 23, a court musician.

2   Sir Francis Weston, aged 25, a friend of Henry and a Gentleman of the Privy Chamber.

3   Sir Henry Norris, aged around 54, a long-term friend of Henry. He held the privileged post of Groom of the Stool.

4   Sir William Brereton, aged around 48, a Gentleman of the Privy Chamber who controlled large areas of the Welsh Marches (see page 9).

5   Most sensationally of all, Anne's own brother, George Boleyn, aged 32, a diplomat and also a member of the Privy Chamber.

Was Anne guilty of the crimes brought against her? She was certainly a flirt who enjoyed male company. However, it is unlikely that these flirtations went beyond this – especially not on the scale of the charges brought against her. With the exception of Mark Smeaton, all four men denied the charges. As a result of their noble status, they could not be tortured and so their claims are more reliable than Smeaton's. Anne, too, protested her innocence.

However, none of this mattered. Henry believed Anne was guilty. He even talked of her having committed adultery with a hundred men. In his mind, she now deserved to die.

Activities ?

1 The date is 15 May 1536. It is the first day of Anne Boleyn's trial for treason and adultery. Sum up the likely views of the following people:
   a Henry VIII
   b Thomas Cromwell
   c Anne Boleyn
   d Jane Seymour.
2 Do you think Anne Boleyn was guilty of the crimes put against her in 1536? Write a paragraph explaining your opinion, using evidence from the text to support your views.

The role of Cromwell

Cromwell played a significant role in bringing down the queen.

- On Henry's behalf, Cromwell looked at whether Anne's former relationship with Henry Percy, son of the Earl of Northumberland, could be used as evidence her marriage to the king was not valid. There were rumours that Anne had been secretly engaged to marry Henry Percy before she married the king. If true, this could be used to argue that Henry's marriage was null and void. However, Cromwell could find no evidence that Anne had been secretly engaged before her marriage to Henry VIII.

- Cromwell took the lead role in building the adultery case against Anne. He personally interrogated Mark Smeaton.
- Cromwell thoroughly investigated the other main suspects and collected evidence against them. This evidence was mainly based on conversations people had supposedly overheard. The evidence against Anne Boleyn relied heavily on court gossip.
- He made sure the ladies-in-waiting who served the imprisoned Anne were spies, who reported back everything she said to Cromwell.

The Cromwell conspiracy

While Cromwell took the leading role in gathering evidence against Anne Boleyn on Henry's orders, there is a debate among historians as to whether his role was actually much larger than this. Was the queen's fall the result of a plot by Cromwell?

There are two sides to this argument. Some historians see Cromwell, rather than Henry, as wanting Anne Boleyn gone from court. They argue that, by 1536, the queen and chief minister had different views on many important matter. Anne wanted the money being made from the Dissolution of the Monasteries* to be used to fund charities and schools. In foreign policy, she also favoured a French alliance. In contrast, Cromwell wanted to keep the money for the Crown, and preferred an alliance with Charles V and the Habsburg Empire.

Key term

Dissolution of the Monasteries*
The closure of English monasteries by Henry VIII, 1536–40 (see page 79).

Cromwell knew what a dangerous enemy Anne could be. She had, after all, helped bring about the downfall of his former master, Wolsey. Cromwell was determined not to share this fate. As shown in Interpretation 1, there is evidence to suggest that Cromwell resorted to plotting. He spoke to the king about Anne's alleged affairs, knowing it would be sure to bring about the queen's ruin. Henry was therefore manipulated by his cunning chief minister.

Interpretation 1

Thomas Cromwell, The untold story of Henry VIII's most faithful servant by Tracy Borman (2015) sees Cromwell, rather than Henry, as the man behind Anne Boleyn's downfall.

Cromwell knew that he had to construct a watertight case against her: the fact that she had failed to give Henry a son was insufficient basis for a divorce. Neither could he find some religious justification to prove her marriage to the king had been invalid. Besides, an annulment was not enough: to be sure of his own survival, Cromwell had to destroy Anne and her faction totally. She had proved too many times in the past how skilful she was at wheedling her way back into the king's favour. What Cromwell needed was incontrovertible [solid] proof that she was a traitor. The queen herself provided the perfect inspiration. Anne had always been known for her flirtatious manner, and she loved to surround herself with a coterie [group] of male admirers… .

However, this idea of a plot by Cromwell is **not** convincing.

- It is doubtful that Cromwell could have manipulated the king in this way. By now, Henry was a mature and experienced ruler.
- It raises the question: if Cromwell was in a position to manipulate the king, why could he simply not have persuaded Henry to ignore Anne Boleyn's advice on policy?
- Although Cromwell and Anne did have differences, they also had strong areas of agreement, such as their views on Protestantism. Both wanted to see Protestant reforms introduced into the English Church (see page 67).
- It would have been extremely dangerous for Cromwell to have suggested to the king that Anne was being unfaithful based on very little evidence.

Instead, Cromwell can be seen as Henry's loyal assistant. He only became involved in bringing about the queen's downfall when asked to by the king.

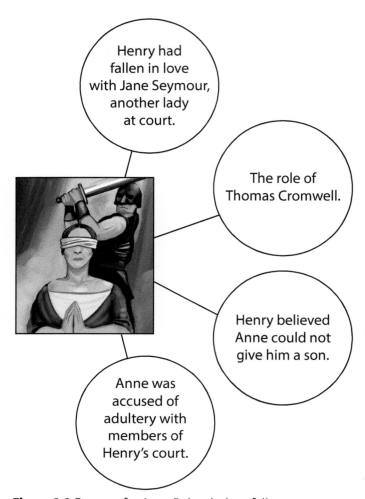

Figure 2.3 Reasons for Anne Boleyn's downfall.

Henry had fallen in love with Jane Seymour, another lady at court.

The role of Thomas Cromwell.

Henry believed Anne could not give him a son.

Anne was accused of adultery with members of Henry's court.

Anne Boleyn's arrest and execution

Anne's fall took less than three weeks. On 2 May, she was arrested and sent to the Tower of London. On 15 May, she was tried jointly with her brother before 26 noblemen. Her uncle, the Duke of Norfolk, was the presiding judge. Anne pleaded her innocence, but was found guilty and sentenced to death.

On 17 May, the Archbishop of Canterbury annulled Henry's marriage to Anne. Despite being one of Anne's firm supporters, he had to follow the king's orders. Princess Elizabeth was therefore made illegitimate and lost her direct claim to the throne.

On 19 May, Anne was led from the Tower to the awaiting executioner. It was a public spectacle, with a crowd of 1,000 people watching. As Source B shows, Anne used her final words to declare her love for Henry. According to the conventions of the time, it was considered undignified to protest your innocence before you were executed. Many people used the time to admit their guilt. Pointedly, Anne chose to ignore this second 'rule' and did not admit to the crimes she was accused of.

Source B

Anne Boleyn's execution speech, made to a crowd assembled at the Tower of London on 19 May, 1536.

Good Christian people, I have not come here to preach a sermon, I have come here to die. For according to the law and by the law I am judged to die, and therefore I will speak nothing against it. I am come hither to accuse no man, nor to speak of that whereof I am accused and condemned to die, but I pray God save the King and send him long to reign over you, for a gentler nor a more merciful prince was there never, and to me he was ever a good, a gentle and sovereign lord. And if any person will meddle of my cause, I require them to judge the best. And thus I take my leave of the world and of you all, and I heartily desire you all to pray for me.

Activities

1   In small groups, discuss the following statement: 'If circumstances had been different and Anne Boleyn had given Henry a male heir, her position would have been secure'.

2   Split the class into two groups, and take it in turns to argue each side. To prepare for this, each group must nominate a spokesperson to argue their case.

3   Read Anne's final speech in Source B. What message do you think Anne wanted to send to Henry and to the English people?

Exam-style question, Section B

Explain why Anne Boleyn fell from her position as Henry's queen. You may use the following in your answer:

- the succession
- Jane Seymour.

You **must** also use information of your own. **12 marks**

Exam tip

Top level answers need to be analytical. This means that, instead of describing Anne Boleyn's imprisonment and execution, you need to give distinct reasons to explain its cause.

Jane Seymour: marriage, heir and death

As soon as Henry heard the news of Anne Boleyn's execution, he went to visit Jane Seymour. The next day, he asked her to marry him. The wedding, a small, private affair, took place on 30 May 1536. The swiftness of the marriage reflected Henry's urgent need for a son. By now, there was a growing sense of unease about the future of the Tudor line. With both his previous marriages declared invalid and his two daughters, Mary and Elizabeth, made illegitimate, there was no legitimate heir to the throne.

It is likely that Henry's back-up plan was to make his illegitimate son, Henry Fitzroy, heir to the throne. To allow this, parliament passed a **Succession Act** giving the king the power to appoint any successor at any time. However, Fitzroy died soon after this Act was passed.

All hopes now rested on wife number three. Jane adopted the motto 'bound to obey and serve'. She was gentle, kind and not overly bright. In short, she was the ideal wife for the middle-aged Henry. Above all, she fulfilled her role as a wife of the king of England by giving birth to the future Edward VI on 12 October 1537. Henry had at last achieved his wish of securing the succession. The rejoicing, however, was short lived. The birth had been difficult, lasting three days, and Jane died less than two weeks later. Henry was deeply saddened. He wore black for the next three months and did not remarry for over two years.

THINKING HISTORICALLY   Cause and Consequence (3c&d)

Causation and intention

1 Work on your own, or with a partner, to identify as many causes of the execution of Anne Boleyn as you can. Write each cause on a separate card or piece of paper.

2 Divide your cards into those that represent:

   a the actions or intentions of people

   b the beliefs held by people at the time

   c the contextual factors: e.g. political, social or economic events

   d states of affairs (long-term situations that have developed over time).

3 Focus on the intentions and actions of the key people in the run-up to Anne Boleyn's fall: Anne Boleyn herself, Henry VIII, Thomas Cromwell, the Duke of Norfolk, Jane Seymour. For each person, draw on your knowledge to fill in a table, identifying:

   a their intentions in 1536

   b the actions they took to achieve these

   c the consequences of their actions (both intended and unintended)

   d the extent to which their intentions were achieved.

4 Discuss the following questions with a partner:

   a Did any one party intend for Anne Boleyn to be executed in 1536?

   b How important are people's intentions in explaining Anne Boleyn's execution?

The influence of the Seymours

As queen, Jane did not challenge the king regularly or get involved in politics. One of the few exceptions was when she pleaded with Henry to spare those who had taken part in a rebellion against her husband's religious policies, known as the Pilgrimage of Grace (see page 85). His reply was to threaten her with Anne's fate. Jane had more success in helping reconcile Henry and his rejected daughter, Princess Mary. However, it was firmly on his terms. Mary had to beg his forgiveness and accept that her mother, Catherine of Aragon, had never truly been his wife.

Jane was from a politically established family. She was born to Margery Wentworth and Sir John Seymour, a courtier who had served both Henry VII and Henry VIII. In total, the couple had ten children, including Jane. When she became queen, she enhanced their status and influence. Although Jane died just one year and four months into her marriage, the fact that she had provided Henry with a son ensured the Seymour family remained important members of court for the rest of Henry's reign.

Jane's eldest brother, Edward Seymour, was the most successful of the Seymours. He was made Earl of Hertford just three days after Edward was born. He then became a leading adviser to Henry.

Extend your knowledge

Henry Fitzroy (1519–36)

Born to Henry's mistress, Elizabeth Blount, Henry Fitzroy was officially acknowledged by Henry as his son. In fact, the surname 'Fitzroy' is an Anglo-Norman name meaning 'son of the king'.

In 1525, Henry made Fitzroy the Duke of Richmond. This was significant. It was the first time since the 12th century that an illegitimate son had been made a duke, and it shows that Fitzroy was being considered as a potential heir. However, fate intervened. He died in July 1536, aged 17, possibly of tuberculosis.

The arrangements for his funeral are revealing. Henry ordered Fitzroy's body to be wrapped in lead, instead of being placed in an ornate royal coffin. He was then hidden in a wagon under straw and taken for a secret burial, supervised by the Duke of Norfolk. It is likely that Henry did not want to draw attention to another lost heir.

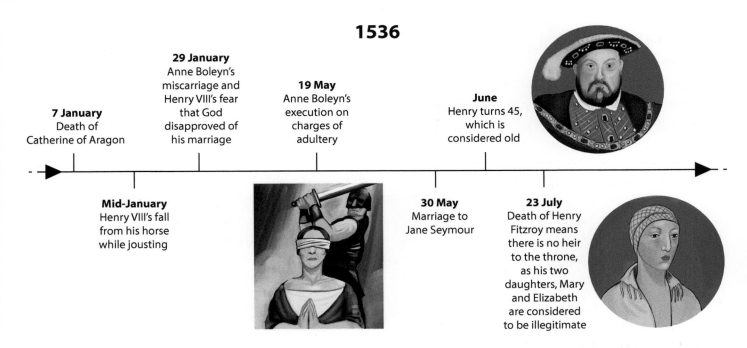

1536

7 January
Death of Catherine of Aragon

29 January
Anne Boleyn's miscarriage and Henry VIII's fear that God disapproved of his marriage

19 May
Anne Boleyn's execution on charges of adultery

June
Henry turns 45, which is considered old

Mid-January
Henry VIII's fall from his horse while jousting

30 May
Marriage to Jane Seymour

23 July
Death of Henry Fitzroy means there is no heir to the throne, as his two daughters, Mary and Elizabeth are considered to be illegitimate

Figure 2.4 The significance of 1536.

Exam-style question, Section B

Describe **two** features of the Seymour family. **4 marks**

Exam tip

To gain full marks on this question, you need to back up both features with relevant historical knowledge.

Activities

In small groups, study Figure 2.4 and discuss why 1536 was a highly significant year in Henry's life. Which event was the most significant, and which was the least significant? Write a paragraph explaining your answer.

You may wish to come back to this timeline once you have studied the Pilgrimage of Grace in chapter 3.

Summary

- After six years of waiting, Henry VIII finally married Anne Boleyn in January 1533. In May 1536, she was found guilty of treason and adultery, and was beheaded.
- Anne Boleyn fell from power mainly because she had failed to provide Henry with a son.
- By 1536, the king had fallen in love with Jane Seymour.
- Henry's chief minister, Cromwell, played a key role in bringing down Anne Boleyn by gathering evidence against her.
- Jane Seymour gave birth to the future king, Edward VI. The succession was now secure, although Jane died soon after giving birth.
- Once Jane was queen, and even after her death, the Seymour family played an influential role in Henry's government.

Checkpoint

Strengthen

S1 List the four main reasons for the fall of Anne Boleyn.

S2 Describe what happened to Anne Boleyn between 2 May and 19 May, 1536.

S3 Describe the type of queen Jane Seymour was.

Challenge

C1 Why was pressure mounting on Henry to secure the succession by 1536?

C2 To what extent were the reasons for Catherine of Aragon and Anne Boleyn's fall similar?

C3 How much responsibility should be attached to Cromwell for the fall of Anne Boleyn?

How confident do you feel about your answers to these questions? Re-read the section on the fall of Anne Boleyn and write a summary of the key points. Share your answers with a classmate. Have you noted the same points?

Learning outcomes

- Understand Cromwell's reforms of government and royal finances.
- Understand why Cromwell believed Henry's government needed reforming.

When Cromwell was arrested in 1540, all his notes and papers were confiscated and preserved. These included draft letters and scribbled notes, as well as a series of documents where Cromwell recorded all the ideas that he wished to discuss with the king. Using these, historians can see the huge role played by Cromwell in developing Tudor government and finance.

Some of the major contributions made by Cromwell included:

- reforms to the Royal Council
- strengthening the Council of the North

- limiting the role of the Kings Chamber in handling financial matters
- expanding the role of parliament.

Reforms of government and royal finance

Over the course of the 1530s, Cromwell set out to improve the way England was governed. His main method for doing this was to impose rules and regulations on institutions that previously had none.

The Royal Council

The Royal Council was an important advisory body to the king, and took a key role in the day-to-day running of the country. However, Cromwell realised that it needed change, as there were many problems to be fixed.

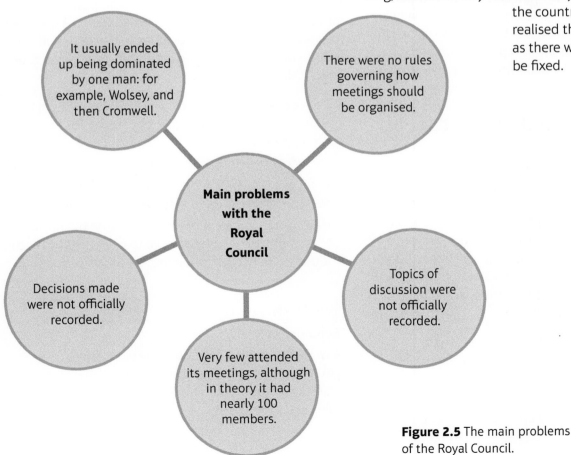

Figure 2.5 The main problems of the Royal Council.

Cromwell created a new, simpler version of the Royal Council known as the **Privy Council**. It was made up of 20 permanent advisers. Most were lawyers and professional administrators rather than untrained members of the nobility and clergy. Cromwell hoped this would stop one personality dominating the Privy Council, as all members would have similar working experience. A clerk of the Privy Council was also appointed to record decisions.

One system of government

Another aim of Cromwell was to create one uniform system of government for the whole of Henry's kingdom. The north of England, in particular, had a long tradition of independence. Under the 1536 Act, abolishing Franchises and Liberties, the north came under firm royal control. The **Council of the North**, a royal body first set up in 1472 to improve how the north of England was governed, was also strengthened. It was made into a permanent institution, and given responsibility for maintaining law and order.

Most significantly, Cromwell guided the **Act of Union** through parliament in 1536. Wales was now formally a part of England. Under its terms, English law replaced Welsh law and Wales was given representation in parliament. It was also divided into counties, as England was, each one headed by a Justice of the Peace.

Reforming the role of the King's Chamber

Cromwell also turned his considerable ability to Henry VIII's financial system. Each year, significant amounts of money went in (income) and out (expenditure) of the Crown's treasury. Officials in the King's Chamber were in charge of keeping track of this. The King's Chamber was located in the Royal Household itself, and supposedly meant the king could keep a close eye on income and expenditure. However, by the mid-1530s, Cromwell recognised this system was in need of reform for three main reasons.

1   Routine tasks, such as keeping a close eye on expenditure and income, bored Henry and so he rarely got involved.

2   There were no formal rules outlining how the King's Chamber should be run. Accounts were not properly kept or checked.

3   The dissolution of the monasteries (see page 79) led to a dramatic increase in Crown income and the King's Chamber would not be able to cope.

Because of these problems, Cromwell decided to remove most of the King's Chamber's financial responsibilities.

The Court of Augmentations and the Court of First Fruits and Tenths

To tackle these problems, Cromwell created a number of new government departments, each looking after a specific area of revenue. The two most significant were:

* the **Court of Augmentations**, created in 1536, which dealt with property and income gained from the dissolution of the monasteries

* the **Court of First Fruits and Tenths**, created in 1540, which collected a tax from the clergy that had previously been sent to Rome.

As these departments had legal powers to settle financial disputes over how much was owed, they were called courts rather than departments.

These reforms should be seen as an important step forward in how England was governed because Cromwell was developing what we would recognise as a modern bureaucracy*. This is how countries are largely run today. Specifically:

* each department, or court, received money from a specific source and only paid out money for pre-approved reasons

* each department was routinely and carefully checked to ensure that they were acting appropriately

* each department was staffed by well-trained officials

* by moving significant powers away from the Royal Household, Henry did not have to be as involved in the routine task of monitoring income and expenditure.

Key term

Bureaucracy*

A way of managing a country. The work of the government is split into different departments, each staffed by officials who work according to agreed rules and procedures.

The management and use of parliament

Today, parliament – made up of the House of Commons and the House of Lords – forms a foundation for the British government. It has the power to make statute law* covering all areas of life.

> **Key term**
>
> **Statute law***
>
> An Act of Parliament that has been agreed by both houses and signed by the monarch. An act which has not yet been approved by parliament is known as a **bill**.

> **Extend your knowledge**
>
> **The history of parliament**
> Simon de Montfort called the first parliament in the 13th century.

For a good deal of Henry's reign, however, parliament was a minor institution, summoned only occasionally to approve new taxation. In an age of personal monarchy, there was little need for it. Henry reached decisions with his chief minister and other trusted advisers, and new laws were usually made by royal proclamation.

Cromwell saw the potential to bring about ground breaking changes through statute law. He did not want to rely on Henry's personal monarchy style of rule. The king's divorce from Catherine of Aragon is a good example of Cromwell's changes through statute law, as it was only made possible by the Act in Restraint of Appeals.

> **Extend your knowledge**
>
> **The extent of parliamentary laws**
> Even more far-reaching than Henry's divorce, laws passed by parliament were used to break with Rome and establish an independent English Church (see page 70).

Parliament began passing an increasing number of laws. Only 203 Acts were passed between 1509 and 1531 – mainly on taxation. However, between 1532 and 1540, 333 Acts were passed. Parliament also met more frequently.

Therefore, a key change had occurred. Cromwell used parliament much more than it had been used before, and made it a partner in government. This was deliberate.

- The House of Lords, mainly made up of peers and bishops, represented the nobility and the Church.
- The House of Commons, containing 74 county MPs and 236 town and borough MPs, was made up of wealthy landowners, merchants and royal administrators.

Cromwell realised that parliament was his way of securing support from the people who mattered. They would be more willing to support decisions if they were involved in approving them.

Not that Cromwell was prepared to leave parliamentary approval to chance. He used various strategies to make sure that MPs were well managed and did exactly what he and the king wanted.

- As the king's chief minister, he controlled parliamentary business, ensuring that his proposals were put forward and discussed.
- As an elected MP, he sat in the House of Commons, so was able to guide significant debates personally.
- As a skilled lawyer, he personally drafted many of the laws put before parliament.
- In 1532, when supporters of Catherine of Aragon were opposing the Act of Annates*, the king visited parliament. As intended, his presence successfully intimidated the Commons into supporting the law.

> **Key term**
>
> **Act of Annates***
>
> This banned the payment of a tax to Rome from the salaries of recently appointed clergy.

In managing parliament, Cromwell was helped by his long experience as an MP – he was first elected in 1523. He was also helped by the fact that many Members of Parliament saw themselves as loyal subjects, and wanted to support laws put forward in the king's name.

Figure 2.6 'King in Parliament'.

Cromwell's use of parliament had important implications. It helped develop the idea that:

- Parliament was a key part of government and should be consulted on major matters of reform.
- Parliament could pass laws on virtually any aspect of life.
- The highest laws of the kingdom were not those made by the king alone, but by the king with the approval of the House of Commons and House of Lords. This is best summed up by the phrase '**King in Parliament**'.

It was not his intention, but Cromwell had nudged England towards a more modern system of parliamentary government.

Exam-style question, Section B

'The main changes to Henry VIII's system of government and finance in the years 1534–40 was a greater role for parliament'.

How far do you agree? Explain your answer.

You may use the following in your answer:

- Statue Law
- government departments.

You **must** also use information of your own. **16 marks**

Exam tip

To do well in this question, you need to provide an analytical answer. Include accurate and relevant historical knowledge, identify one additional point beyond those given in the question, and reach an overall judgement in a conclusion.

Summary

- Cromwell wanted to improve the way Henry VIII's kingdom was governed.
- To take on the routine tasks of running the country, he developed a smaller Privy Council out of the existing Royal Council.
- To administer the kingdom's finances, he created a series of government departments, staffed by well-trained administrators, and with set rules and procedures to follow.
- The most important of these were the Court of Augmentations and the Court of First Fruits and Tenths.
- Cromwell also aimed at bringing remote areas of the kingdom under firmer royal control.
- The 1536 Act of Union formally placed Wales under English rule.
- The role of parliament increased significantly under Cromwell. He used it to secure the backing of the political nation for many of his far-reaching policies.

Checkpoint

Strengthen

S1 Describe the changes made to the Royal Council in the 1530s.

S2 Describe the two main financial departments created by Cromwell.

S3 Outline three ways in which Cromwell's use of parliament was new.

Challenge

C1 Why do you think Cromwell wanted to change the government and financial system of Henry's kingdom?

C2 In what ways was the concept of personal monarchy eroded by Cromwell's reforms?

C3 In what ways could parliament claim to represent the political nation?

How confident do you feel about your answers to these questions? Share your answers with a partner and see if you can improve them together.

Timeline

Key events in the downfall of Cromwell

Early 1539 Invasion scare in England

March 1539 Marriage negotiations with the Cleves family are opened

6 January 1540 Henry VIII and Anne of Cleves are married

24 June 1540 Anne of Cleves is ordered to leave court

9 July 1540 Henry's fourth marriage is annulled

10 June 1540 Thomas Cromwell is arrested for treason and heresy

28 July 1540 Thomas Cromwell is executed and Henry marries Catherine Howard

Reasons for Henry's marriage to Anne of Cleves

The question of Henry's marriage was highly political. His privy councillors had started the search for a new bride only days after Jane Seymour died.

By 1539, Anne of Cleves, the second daughter of the Duke of Cleves, had emerged as the favourite. Anne was gentle, virtuous and obedient – qualities that made her a suitable wife for Henry.

Also, the Cleves family actually wanted Anne to marry Henry – unlike many other families, who had heard of Henry's reputation for mistreating his wives.

For Cleves (a small kingdom in the north of the Holy Roman Empire) the marriage offered the chance to make an alliance with a great European power. And England, with the threat of invasion a real possibility, needed friends. Cleves seemed a good choice for an ally as, like England, it had expelled the authority of the pope, but had not replaced it with Protestantism.

Fifteen thirty nine started in panic. It was feared that Francis I of France and Charles V of Spain were about to launch a Catholic crusade to invade England. Spies reported fleets gathering in the great ports of Antwerp and Boulogne, as well as an army in the Netherlands.

The south-east coast of England became a frenzy of activity, as this was the most probable site for an enemy invasion. Troops were trained, defences strengthened and ammunition collected. Henry toured the area, visiting his fleet at Portsmouth on 8 May. He also oversaw his army marching through London.

Cromwell saw another way to save England other than force: marrying Henry to a potential ally against Spain and France.

Source A

This portrait of Anne of Cleves was painted by Hans Holbein in 1539.

Cromwell also had his own private motives for encouraging the union. An alliance with a state such as Cleves would mean he could make more religious reforms without opposition from a Catholic queen (see the table on page 77 to find out more about Cromwell's religious reforms). A foreign princess would also lack connections to the great English noble families, and so was less likely to be used to attack him.

Despite Cromwell's active involvement, the ultimate choice should still be seen as Henry's. He would not have let his chief minister decide on a matter as important as this. Correspondence between the two also showed that Cromwell was responding to orders and the king was very much in control.

In March 1539, Henry agreed that marriage negotiations could begin. A treaty confirming the match was signed on 4 October 1539.

Timeline
England's isolation

June 1538 Charles V and Francis I meet at Nice and sign a ten-year truce

December 1538 Pope Paul III issues a bull of excommunication, stating that Henry was no longer part of the Catholic Church and should be removed as king

January 1539 Francis I and Charles V sign a further pact at Toledo, promising not to enter into any agreement with England without the others consent

Figure 2.7 Reasons for Henry's marriage to Anne of Cleves.

The significance of the marriage

Henry's marriage to Anne of Cleves was significant for five main reasons.

1 It showed that Henry and his advisers, despite the birth of Edward, were still worried about the succession. Henry wanted more sons.

2 Anne of Cleves was not Henry's first choice of bride. Many families would not allow their daughters to marry someone who had a reputation for killing his wives. This shows how much Henry's reputation had been tarnished by his actions against Catherine of Aragon and Anne Boleyn.

3 Henry's need to ally himself with a small state like Cleves showed the level of England's isolation in Europe.

4 The marriage suggested that Henry had no intention of reversing his decision to break from the Roman Catholic Church, as Cleves had also broken with Rome.

5 Cromwell had played a key role in bringing about this marriage. His future would now partly depend on how successful it was.

The failure of the marriage and its implications

Anne of Cleves has unfairly gone down in history as the 'Flanders mare', who was so ugly that Henry divorced her within six months. However, it is worth noting that many others were far more complimentary about the young princess. For whatever reason, Henry took an instant dislike to her. He first saw her in December 1539, when she landed in England. 'I like her not! I like her not!' he was famously meant to have shouted at Cromwell.

The wedding was postponed for two days as Henry desperately tried to get out of the marriage. Cromwell persuaded him to go through with it, but Henry must also have realised he had little choice. He needed an alliance: at that moment, Charles V and Francis I were meeting in Paris. For all Henry knew, they were plotting an invasion of England.

The couple were married on 6 January 1540. That night, Henry was unable to consummate the marriage.

The next day, Henry reported to Cromwell that he had 'left her as good a maid as I found her'.

Further factors, besides Anne's looks, soon convinced Henry that the marriage could not last. Anne simply did not fit into the sophisticated court life of England. She was shy by nature, but had also grown up in an uncultured household. Anne's education, under the control of her mother, centred on needlework and household management. The skills which would have allowed her to pass in the English court – such as singing, dancing, playing musical instruments and languages – had simply not been taught, because in Cleves they were considered unnecessary for a young lady.

Catherine Howard

Source B

A portrait of a lady believed to be Catherine Howard, painted by Hans Holbein in 1540.

In addition, Henry had now fallen in love with Catherine Howard, a lady-in-waiting to Anne of Cleves. Catherine was young and flirty. Henry started pursuing her seriously in the spring of 1540. By this point, it had also become evident that an alliance with the state of Cleves was no longer needed, as relations between Francis I and Charles V had broken down.

This change in international relations was something Cromwell had no control over. However, its implications were significant, both for the king's marriage and for Cromwell's fall from power. With no foreign policy considerations to hold Henry back, the king took action. By the start of July, his marriage had been annulled on the grounds of non-consummation and the existence of a prior marriage contract between Anne and the Duke of Lorraine. By the end of the month, Catherine Howard was his fifth wife.

In return for Anne of Cleve's meek acceptance of the annulment, she was richly rewarded with several manor houses, including Hever Castle, the former home of Anne Boleyn. She was also given a considerable annual income, and granted official status as the king's 'sister'. This made her more important than all of Henry's other subjects – except his children and any future wife.

For Cromwell, in contrast, the outcome was deadly.

Activity ?

Carry out further research into the six wives of Henry VIII. Who do you think can claim to have been the most successful of his wives? Why?

Cromwell's fall from power

Henry blamed Cromwell for the failure of his marriage to Anne of Cleves – who Henry now believed should never have been brought to England in the first place – and wanted to punish him. Also, by this stage, Henry had already started to lose faith in Cromwell as a result of his religious policies. Over the course of the 1530s, the chief minister steadily advanced the Protestant cause. But despite breaking from Rome, and showing some sympathy to reformist ideas, Henry still thought of himself as a Catholic. By the late 1530s, he was demanding a return to traditional Catholic values.

While Cromwell was weakened by these events, his fall from power was not certain. In April 1540, he was awarded the title Earl of Essex – he was now a member of the nobility. For a Putney 'ruffian' with no aristocratic blood, this was a rare honour and suggests a significant degree of ongoing support from Henry. Indeed, Cromwell might well have survived had it not been for the actions of the Duke of Norfolk.

The influence of the Duke of Norfolk

Thomas Howard, the Duke of Norfolk, had spent much of the 1530s competing with Cromwell for influence over Henry. Norfolk hated Cromwell for three main reasons.

1 While Cromwell supported Protestant ideas, Norfolk was a Catholic.

2 Norfolk believed that Cromwell should not be allowed to advise the king because of his low birth.

3 Norfolk was angry when Cromwell was made Earl of Essex. Norfolk did not think a commoner should have such an important title.

By 1540, Norfolk realised that he was at last in a position to destroy his enemy.

- He saw that Cromwell's power was fading as a result of Henry's anger regarding Anne of Cleves, and his concern about Cromwell's religious beliefs.
- Catherine Howard was Norfolk's niece, and this gave Norfolk huge influence over the king.

Norfolk's strategy was to poison Cromwell's reputation with Henry. Early in 1540, he instructed Catherine Howard to spread rumours that he was not putting enough effort into securing the divorce from Anne of Cleves. He then claimed that Cromwell was plotting to introduce Protestantism to England fully, knowing that Henry fiercely opposed this idea.

Both accusations were untrue. Cromwell was extremely good at his work and completely dedicated to serving Henry. He showed no desire to carry out policies against the king's wishes. Unfortunately for Cromwell, Henry was angry and he chose to believe what Norfolk said.

He was born into a powerful and long established noble family. He was an experienced soldier. For example, in 1513, he helped defeat the Scots at the battle of Flodden.

He held many important positions in Henry's government, including Lord of Ireland in 1520, Lord Treasurer in 1524 and Earl Marshal in 1533.

He helped bring about Cromwell's downfall in 1540 and emerged for a short-time as the second most powerful man in England.

He failed in his aim to become Henry's chief minister.

In the 1530s, he opposed Cromwell, hating his background and religious views.

He was the uncle of Anne Boleyn and Catherine Howard, and he played a major role in bringing about their marriages to Henry. This further increased his influence in Henry's court.

In the 1520s, he had been the enemy of Cardinal Wolsey, despising him for his lowly origins and reluctance to go to war.

He was a firm Roman Catholic and eventually fell out with Anne Boleyn as a result of her Protestant religious views. Howard presided over her trial and the five men accused with her.

Figure 2.8 Facts about Thomas Howard, the 3rd Duke of Norfolk (1473–1554).

Activity ?

Henry's court was full of ambitious nobles, looking for adventure and to make a name for themselves. As well as the Duke of Norfolk, Charles Brandon, Nicholas Carew, Thomas Wyatt, William Carey, Henry Howard and Thomas Seymour were also important.

Pick one or two of these men for further research and compile your own top facts about them.

Key terms

Heresy*

A religious view which went against official opinion. Cromwell was charged with being a devout Protestant, which conflicted with the Catholic beliefs of the king.

Act of Attainder*

An Act of Parliament that declares a person guilty of treason with no requirement to prove it in court through a trial.

Cromwell was well aware of the danger posed by Norfolk. He retaliated in many different ways.

In February 1540, Cromwell ordered the closure of Thetford Priory in Norfolk. This was a very personal attack on the Duke of Norfolk, as the priory was an important location for the Duke. He had planned to use it as a college for priests. It was also his family burial place. Cromwell made sure the priory was completely destroyed, which meant that Norfolk had to arrange for his ancestors' bones to be dug up and reburied elsewhere.

Cromwell also tried to have Norfolk exiled from court, claiming that he had been in contact with a sufferer of sweating sickness. However, Norfolk successfully persuaded Henry that he was not infected.

But, in the end, time simply ran out for Cromwell.

The execution of Thomas Cromwell

Cromwell's end came swiftly. On 10 June 1540, he was arrested at a Privy Council meeting on charges of treason and heresy*. Norfolk is reported to have ripped Cromwell's decorations of state from around his neck. Protesting that he was no traitor, Cromwell was taken to the Tower of London. Meanwhile, royal officials seized his goods, which were valued at £7,000 (£2 million today). On 29 June, parliament passed an Act of Attainder* condemning the chief minister to death. Cromwell had used this against others and knew what it meant. He would not be entitled to a trial to clear his name.

Cromwell now wrote for his life. His only chance of survival rested on persuading the king of his innocence. Part of his letter to Henry can be seen in Source C.

Source C

An extract from Cromwell's last letter to Henry VIII, dated 30 June 1540. For a calm and calculating man, Cromwell's desperation is clear.

...beseeching most humbly your Grace to pardon this my rude writing, and to consider that I am a most woeful prisoner, ready to take the death, when it shall please God and your Majesty; and yet the frail flesh inciteth me continually to call to your Grace for mercy and pardon for mine offences; and thus Christ save, preserve and keep you. Written at the Tower this Wednesday, the last of June, with the heavy heart and trembling hand of your Highness's most heavy and most miserable prisoner and poor slave,

Thomas Cromwell

Most gracious Prince, I cry for mercy, mercy, mercy!

The king, however, offered no mercy. His one-time adviser and friend was beheaded on 28 July 1540. On the same day, Henry married Catherine Howard.

There would be no more advisers to Henry with the same influence as Wolsey or Cromwell. For the remainder of his reign, Henry chose to rule alone, rather than promoting another chief minister.

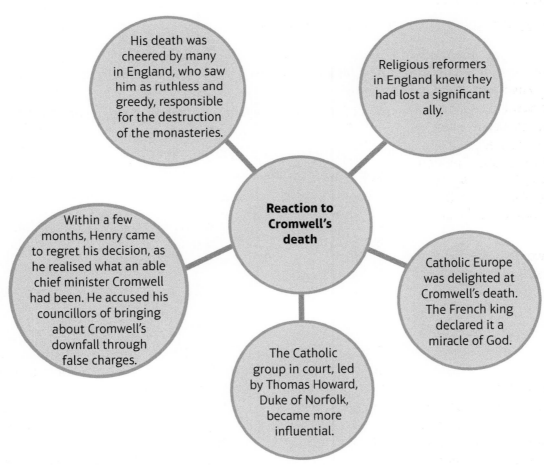

Figure 2.9 Reactions to Cromwell's death.

Summary

- Henry's advisers encouraged him to remarry after the death of Jane Seymour.
- England was diplomatically isolated by the Catholic powers and needed new allies. It was hoped that the marriage to Anne of Cleves could provide this.
- The marriage only lasted six months. Henry was not physically attracted to Anne of Cleves and instead fell in love with Catherine Howard, one of Anne's ladies-in-waiting.
- The failure of the king's marriage to Anne of Cleves was a key reason for the fall of Cromwell. The king wanted to punish him.
- The Duke of Norfolk played a significant role in bringing Cromwell down.

Checkpoint

Strengthen

S1 Note down three reasons for the failure of Henry's marriage to Anne of Cleves.

S2 Name two reasons why the Duke of Norfolk hated Cromwell.

S3 Name the legal instrument used to bring Cromwell down.

Challenge

C1 A need for a son, or the need to protect his kingdom: which reason do you think most influenced Henry in his decision to marry Anne of Cleves and why?

C2 Why do you think Anne of Cleves did not suffer the same fate as Catherine of Aragon or Anne Boleyn when her marriage collapsed?

C3 What are the similarities and differences between Wolsey's and Cromwell's falls?

How confident do you feel about your answers to these questions? Share your answers with a partner and see if you can improve them together.

Recap Henry VIII and Cromwell, 1529–40

Recall quiz

1 When did Cromwell first enter parliament?
2 What was the public reason for Anne Boleyn's execution?
3 Who did Henry VIII marry after Anne Boleyn?
4 Why did Henry VIII view his third marriage as a success?
5 Name the two important finance departments established by Cromwell.
6 Which government institution lost a lot of financial power under Cromwell?
7 How many additional Acts of Parliament were passed while Cromwell was chief minister compared to the period of Henry's reign before this?
8 Who was the powerful noble who helped bring about the downfall of Cromwell?
9 What promotion did Cromwell gain just before his fall from power?
10 What other significant event happened on the day of Cromwell's execution?

Exam-style question, Section B

'Thomas Cromwell fell from power because of the actions of the Duke of Norfolk'.

How far do you agree? Explain your answer.

You may use the following in your answer:

- charges of heresy
- Anne of Cleves.

You **must** also use information of your own. **16 marks**

Exam tip

This question requires you to provide an overall judgement. To do this well, you need to discuss the importance of each factor in a conclusion.

Activities

It is time to review Thomas Cromwell's life. To do this, you are going to make an 'achievement graph' for Henry's chief minister. The x axis will show time, from 1509 to his death in 1540. The y axis will show level of achievement, with 10 being a huge success and 0 being a failure. Go back through this chapter and pick out all the key events of Cromwell's life and decide where best to place them on your graph.

1 In small groups, compare your graphs. Did you pick out similar highs and lows?
2 When you read the next chapter and learn more about Cromwell's key religious changes, you will be able to add further details to this graph.

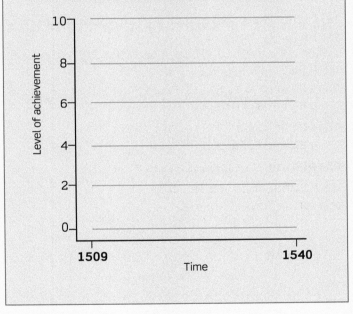

Writing historically: building sentences

Successful historical writing uses a range of sentence structures to achieve clarity, precision and emphasis.

Learning outcomes

By the end of this lesson, you will understand how to:

- use and position subordinate clauses to link ideas with clarity and precision
- manipulate sentence structure to emphasise key ideas.

Definitions

Clause: group of words or unit of meaning that contains a verb and can form part or all of a sentence.
Single clause sentence: sentence containing just one clause.
Subordinating conjunction: a word used to link a dependent clause to the main clause of a sentence.

How can I use sentence structure to link my ideas?

When you are explaining and exploring complex events and ideas, you need to show clearly and precisely how they are linked.

Compare the two drafts of sentences below, written in response to this exam-style question:

> Explain why Cromwell rose to become Henry's chief minister. **(12 marks)**

These points are written in pairs of unlinked, **single clause sentences**.	The relationship between these points is made clear with subordinating conjunctions.
Securing the annulment was key to Cromwell's rise. It ensured Henry's full support.	Securing the annulment was key to Cromwell's rise because it ensured Henry's full support.
Cromwell stayed loyal to Wolsey. Henry appointed him to the Royal Council.	Although Cromwell stayed loyal to Wolsey, Henry appointed him to the Royal Council.
The Act in Restraint of Appeals was passed. Henry had his annulment.	After the Act in Restraint of Appeals was passed, Henry had his annulment.

1. Which responses are more clearly expressed? Write a sentence or two explaining your answer.

Subordinating conjunctions can link ideas to indicate:

- an explanation: (e.g. 'because', 'as', 'in order that')
- a condition: (e.g. 'if', 'unless')
- a comparison: (e.g. 'although', 'whereas')
- a sequence: (e.g. 'when', 'as', 'before', 'until' etc.)

2. In how many different ways can you use subordinating conjunctions to link these pairs of ideas, clearly expressing the relationship between them?

- Cromwell took on Henry's case. He realised there was no point arguing the case in Rome.
- Cromwell argued Henry should take the pope's powers. His court settled the annulment.

How can I structure my sentences for clarity and emphasis?

In sentences where ideas are linked with subordinate conjunctions, there is:

- a main clause that gives the central point of the sentence
- a dependent, subordinate clause that adds more information about that central point.

Different sentence structures can alter the emphasis of your writing. Look at these sentences that have been used to introduce responses to the exam-style question on the previous page.

Compare these two versions of the first sentence:

> *After the Act in Restraint of Appeals was passed, Henry had his annulment.*
> *Cromwell's loyalty impressed Henry and so did his skill.*

This is the main clause in this sentence

This is a subordinate clause. It is linked to the main clause with a subordinating conjunction.

> *Henry had his annulment after the Act in Restraint of Appeals was passed.*
> *Cromwell's loyalty impressed Henry and so did his skill.*

3. Which clause is given more emphasis in each version? Explain your answer.

In both responses, the second sentence in the response above is much shorter than the first sentence:

4. Why do you think the writer chose to make this point in a short sentence? Why does it come after, and not before, the other sentence? Write a sentence or two explaining your ideas.

5. Experiment with different ways of sequencing the three pieces of information in the response above, linking all, some, or none of them with subordinating conjunctions:

> *Cromwell stayed loyal to Wolsey.*
> *Henry appointed Cromwell to the Royal Council.*
>
> *Cromwell's loyalty impressed Henry and so did his skill.*

b. Which version links the ideas most clearly? One of yours or the original version? Write a sentence or two explaining your decision.

Improving an answer

6. Now look at the notes below written in response to the exam-style question on the previous page.

> *Cromwell's loyalty impressed Henry and so did his skill.*
> *The king was in need of talented men.*
> *Cromwell was appointed to the Royal Council.*
> *This placed him in Henry's circle of trusted advisers.*
>
> *Cromwell was ambitious.*
> *He realised that helping Henry to divorce would be sure to gain him promotion.*
> *Henry's nobles were unable to progress Henry's cause.*

a. Experiment with different ways of sequencing and structuring all the information in sentences. Try to write at least three different versions.

b. Which version gives the best historical account? Write a sentence or two explaining your decision.

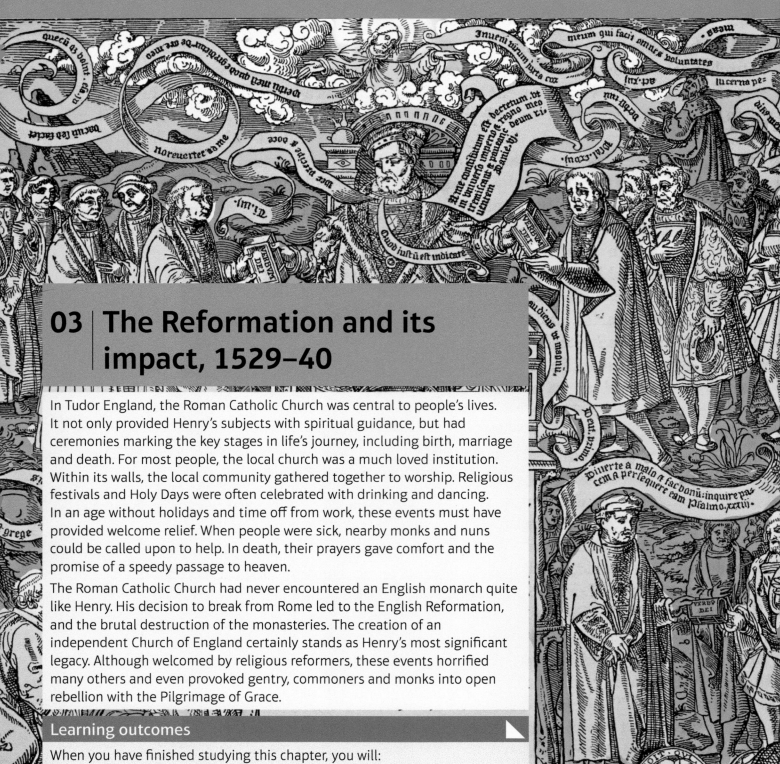

03 | The Reformation and its impact, 1529–40

In Tudor England, the Roman Catholic Church was central to people's lives. It not only provided Henry's subjects with spiritual guidance, but had ceremonies marking the key stages in life's journey, including birth, marriage and death. For most people, the local church was a much loved institution. Within its walls, the local community gathered together to worship. Religious festivals and Holy Days were often celebrated with drinking and dancing. In an age without holidays and time off from work, these events must have provided welcome relief. When people were sick, nearby monks and nuns could be called upon to help. In death, their prayers gave comfort and the promise of a speedy passage to heaven.

The Roman Catholic Church had never encountered an English monarch quite like Henry. His decision to break from Rome led to the English Reformation, and the brutal destruction of the monasteries. The creation of an independent Church of England certainly stands as Henry's most significant legacy. Although welcomed by religious reformers, these events horrified many others and even provoked gentry, commoners and monks into open rebellion with the Pilgrimage of Grace.

Learning outcomes

When you have finished studying this chapter, you will:

- understand why Henry decided to break with Rome and how Cromwell made it happen
- discover how the English Church changed during the Reformation
- understand why the government decided to close the monasteries, and what the impact of these closures was
- understand why Henry lost control of the north of England during the Pilgrimage of Grace and the significance of this uprising.

3.1 The break with Rome

Learning outcomes

- Understand why Henry decided to break away from the Roman Catholic Church.
- Understand the significance of the Act of Succession and Act of Supremacy.
- Understand how Cromwell used Oaths and a Treason Law to prevent people criticising Henry's reforms.

Henry as 'Defender of the Faith'

Henry VIII started his reign as a good Roman Catholic. Like most of the English people, he firmly believed in its teachings (known as **doctrines**) and rituals. These are outlined in the table on page 68. In fact, in 1521, Henry wrote a lengthy book, called *In Defence of the Seven Sacraments*, expressing his support for Roman Catholicism. This earned him the title 'Defender of the Faith' from the pope.

Henry wrote his book to defend the Catholic Church from attacks by a new religious movement, which has since become known as **Protestantism**. Its leading thinker, Martin Luther, was a German priest.

Activity ?

Study Figure 3.1, which shows the interiors of a Roman Catholic and Protestant church. Use your knowledge of each Church's core beliefs to explain the differences.

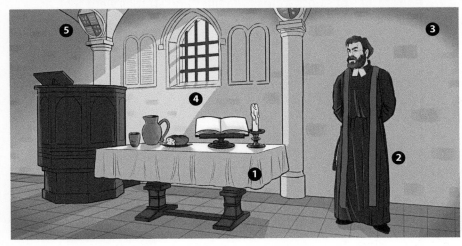

Key
1. Altar, which is set apart from the congregation
2. Ornate robes
3. Painted walls depicting Bible stories
4. Stain glass window
5. Elaborate crucifix and statues of saints

Key
1. Plain table instead of an altar
2. Simple robes
3. No ornate decoration
4. Plain windows
5. Royal crest instead of religious decoration

Figure 3.1 The interiors of a Roman Catholic and Protestant church.

Luther hoped to start a process of reform, or **reformation**, in the Catholic Church. In particular, Luther wanted a Church that was based solely on the teachings of the Bible. This led him to question many aspects of traditional Catholicism.

The table below outlines the differences between Roman Catholicism and Protestantism during Henry's reign.

Key terms

Sacraments*

Special Church ceremonies, including baptism and marriage.

The Eucharist*

Being given bread and wine during a church service in remembrance of The Last Supper.

Transubstantiation*

The belief that bread and wine is transformed into the body and blood of Jesus Christ.

Indulgences*

A certificate issued by the Catholic churches granting a person forgiveness for their sins.

Pilgrimage*

A journey completed for religious reasons.

Roman Catholicism	Protestantism
The pope was head of the Church.	There should be no pope. Instead rulers, such as monarchs, should lead and protect their own churches.
The central function of the Church was to deliver the seven sacraments* as an outward display of devotion to God.	The Church was there to preach the 'Word of the God' through the Bible. Only the three sacraments mentioned in the Bible were valid: baptism, the Eucharist* and penance.
During the Eucharist, it was believed that bread and wine were actually turned into the body and blood of Jesus Christ. This process was called transubstantiation*.	During the Eucharist, bread and wine remained as bread and wine. The service was about remembering Jesus Christ.
Church services and the Bible were in Latin.	Services and the Bible should be in English, to allow ordinary people to understand it for themselves.
Special prayers for the dead could be said to help people get into heaven. Pieces of paper signed by the pope could also be purchased to help. These were called indulgences*.	Praying for the souls of the dead was seen as a waste of time. Indulgences were labelled as corrupt.
Images and statues of saints were worshipped in churches.	Images and statues were seen as superstitious.
Completing a pilgrimage* was seen as a good Catholic duty and a way of gaining God's approval.	Pilgrimages were seen as a waste of time.
Because of their unique role in the Eucharist, priests had a special status, which was reflected in their ornate clothing – known as **vestments**.	Priests were regarded as just ordinary men and did not wear special clothing.

Reasons for Henry's campaign against the pope and the Catholic Church, 1529–33

By 1529, Henry had started an aggressive campaign to increase his power over the English Church at the expense of Rome's.

What pushed Henry into this unlikely course of action? Was it:

- the succession
- new Protestant ideas
- the state of the Church
- just about money?

Henry VIII and the succession

Henry's main concern by 1529 was to divorce Catherine of Aragon. Henry needed this divorce because he thought Catherine could not give him a son and secure the succession (see page 29). Falling in love with Anne Boleyn, and becoming convinced that God disapproved of his marriage to Catherine, only added to his determination to get a divorce.

Henry used the threat of breaking from Rome to pressurise the pope into granting his divorce. Unfortunately for Henry, Pope Clement VII was firmly under the control of Catherine's nephew, Charles V, and was unwilling to grant an annulment.

The impact of Protestantism

Henry was also partly influenced by the spread of new Protestant ideas. Some of the most significant people in his life at this time supported religious reform, including Anne Boleyn, Thomas Cromwell and Thomas Cranmer (who was appointed Archbishop of Canterbury in 1532).

One aspect of Protestantism particularly interested Henry. In 1528, William Tyndale, a leading English Protestant, published the *Obedience of the Christian Man*, arguing that God had always intended the Church to be ruled by kings, rather than the pope. Although the book was banned in England, Anne Boleyn had a copy and gave it to Henry. He was impressed and later said that 'this is the book for me and for all kings'. He believed he should be in charge of every part of England.

However, Henry was not a true Protestant – at heart, he was a Catholic. His dislike of Martin Luther was expressed in his book *In Defence of the Seven Sacraments*. He only believed the parts of Protestantism that suited him.

Anti-Clericalism*

Henry was also partly influenced by a growing concern over the state of the Catholic Church in England. A small minority of ordinary English people, especially merchants and lawyers, felt let down by the Catholic Church (see Figure 3.2).

> **Key term**
>
> **Anti-Clericalism***
> Opposition to the clergy.

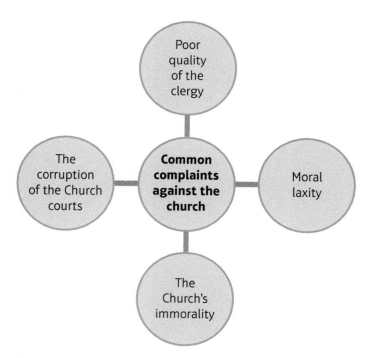

Figure 3.2 Common complaints against the Catholic Church.

Richard Hunne

For many, the case of Richard Hunne summed up all that was wrong with the Catholic Church. Hunne was a London merchant whose baby son died in 1511. After refusing to pay the high funeral fees, Hunne was sued by the local priest, and then arrested on charges of owning Protestant literature. Later, Hunne was found dead, hanging in his cell. Although the authorities claimed suicide, it was suspected that a member of the clergy had murdered him.

However, while a minority were dissatisfied with the Church, most people were generally happy. In fact, many local communities took great pride in their parish churches and raised large sums of money to improve them.

Money

Henry VIII had been involved in a number of expensive wars in Europe. He could not raise enough money by taxes to fund them and was always looking for extra sources of money. The banning of Annates to Rome, for example, suggests that Henry had one eye on revenue. However, the amounts involved were not very big, so money must be seen as more of an extra benefit than a major motivating factor.

The Act of Succession and the Act of Supremacy

The Act of Succession, 1534

- Henry's marriage to Catherine of Aragon was declared invalid. Instead, Anne Boleyn was Henry's lawful wedded wife and queen.
- Only the children of this second marriage would be able to inherit the throne.
- Therefore, Princess Mary, Henry's daughter by Catherine of Aragon, was declared illegitimate and removed from the line of succession.

The significance of the Act of Succession

- It completely changed the order of the succession.
- It established Anne Boleyn's position as queen by law.
- It was a significant step towards the final break with Rome. Henry had now completely rejected the authority of Rome to decide whether he could divorce and remarry. In reply, the pope stated that Henry was still married to Catherine. Henry responded by ordering the pope's name to be struck out of all prayer books in England.

The Act of Supremacy, 1534

The Act of Supremacy was a formal acknowledgment that England was no longer under the pope's control. Henry, rather than the pope, was now head of the English Church, and he had the powers previously held by the pope.

Henry now had the right to decide:

- how the English Church would be organised
- the central beliefs of the English Church
- who would be appointed to the key positions in the English Church.

Henry also made it clear that Cromwell would be a key figure. He was appointed as the King's Vicegerent*, or Vicar General, in spiritual matters, who could also use the powers that legally belonged to the king.

Key term
Vicegerent*
The king's deputy, with responsibility for the day-to-day running of the church.

Source A

An extract from the Act of Supremacy, 1534.

Be it enacted by the authority of this present Parliament, that the King our Sovereign Lord, his heirs and successors, kings of this realm, shall be taken, accepted, and reputed the only Supreme Head in earth of the Church of England.

Source B

An extract from the oath outlined in the Act of Succession, 1534.

To be true to Queen Anne, and to believe and take her for the lawful wife of the King and rightful Queen of England.... ..

The significance of the Act of Supremacy

Although the break with Rome was a dramatic step, its practical significance must not be over stated. In practice, the pope had played a very small part in the affairs of the English Church.

- Although the pope did have the final decision in the appointment of senior members of the clergy, by tradition, he tended to agree with the king.
- Rome was rarely appealed to when disputes were brought before Church courts.
- The basic teachings of the Church were well-established, so Rome did not tell the English Church what to believe.

THINKING HISTORICALLY — Cause and Consequence (4a&b)

Fragile history

Nothing that happens is inevitable. Sometimes things happen due to the actions of an individual or chance events that no one anticipated. Something could have altered or someone could have chosen differently, bringing about a very different outcome.

What actually occurred in the past did happen, but it did not have to be like that.

Working on your own, answer the questions below. When you have answered the questions, discuss the answers in a group. Then have a class vote.

Perceived reasons for Henry VIII's break with Rome

Luther and the rise of Protestantism in Europe	Anti-clerical feeling in England	Henry VIII and Catherine of Aragon's lack of a male heir	The pope denies Henry VIII's request for a divorce	Henry falls in love with Anne Boleyn	Anne Boleyn becomes pregnant	Thomas Cromwell's pro-Protestant outlook

1. Consider Henry's reasons for splitting with Rome.
   a. What might have happened had Henry VIII and Catherine of Aragon had a son? Would all the other causes still be relevant?
   b. What might have happened had the pope granted Henry VIII a divorce?
   c. How did Anne Boleyn's pregnancy influence Henry's decision to break with Rome?

2. Write down any events that you think could be called 'chance events'. How important were these in causing Henry to break with Rome?

3. Imagine you were alive in 1509, when Henry VIII married Catherine of Aragon. Write a paragraph explaining how you think religious practice in England might change in the next 25 years. Remember not to use the benefit of hindsight!

4. Have a class vote: was the break with Rome inevitable? Be prepared to back up your decision.

Cromwell's role in enforcing the Acts

The use of oaths

Henry and Cromwell knew that the radical nature of the Acts of Succession and Supremacy could provoke resistance from the people of England. Their fear was that violent Englishmen might rebel against them.

However, Cromwell, whose job it was to protect Henry from internal threats, believed that only a very small number of people would have the courage to actively resist. Most people who privately believed the Acts were wrong would choose to remain silent in public. However, in the increasingly tense world of Henry's England even people who didn't *openly* resist the Acts were viewed as dangerous.

To combat this, Cromwell turned oath-taking into a powerful weapon. A clause in the Act of Succession required individuals, when asked, to take an oath supporting Anne Boleyn as Henry's queen (see Source B). Refusal would mean punishment as a traitor: this was called the **Oath of Succession**.

This was no empty threat. All of England's political and religious leaders were asked to take this oath. Their response to this request, made it very clear which of them were not prepared to support the changes.

The Treason Act

Cromwell realised that the existing Treason Act of 1352 did not have enough detail for Henry's needs. It defined treason in the traditional way (such as plotting the king's death, waging war against him or helping his enemies), but was not useful for punishing those who spoke out against the king's divorce or the break with Rome.

Cromwell's solution was the 1534 Treason Act, which promised death to anyone denying the royal supremacy. No evidence of a plot or intent to cause the king harm was needed. This marked a dramatic increase in the state's power to deal with its opponents. It also served to frighten those who might be tempted to speak out.

Summary

- Henry started his reign as a strong supporter of the Roman Catholic Church and was rewarded with the title 'Defender of the Faith'.
- In order to secure his divorce from Catherine of Aragon, Henry conducted an aggressive campaign against the Catholic Church.
- Henry's campaign was also partly influenced by the reformist views of his closest advisers, anti-clerical views and money.
- In 1534, The Act of Succession declared Henry's marriage to Catherine of Aragon invalid, while the Act of Supremacy marked the formal break with Rome.
- To make people support these new Acts, they were asked to take oaths, and a new treason law was passed to deal with any resistance.

Checkpoint

Strengthen

S1 Describe how Henry made the final break with Rome in 1534.

S2 Describe how Cromwell used oaths to enforce the Acts of Succession and Supremacy.

Challenge

C1 What were the main differences between Roman Catholics and Protestants in Tudor times?

C2 Which do you think was more significant in increasing Henry's power: the Act of Supremacy or the Act of Succession?

How confident do you feel about your answers to these questions? If you are not sure, it might help to discuss your ideas with other students.

3.2 Opposition to, and impact of, the Reformation, 1534–40

- Understand what happened to Elizabeth Barton and John Fisher when they opposed Henry's religious reforms.
- Understand the significance of Thomas More's opposition to the Reformation.
- Understand how the English Church changed, 1534–40.

Heaven and hell were an important part of everyday life for everyone living in Tudor England. Therefore, to avoid eternal damnation, the right spiritual choices had to be made. This is why Henry's decision to break with Rome was so important to his subjects: they believed he was playing with the fate of their souls.

Surprisingly, given the significance of the religious changes, most people in England seem to have accepted them. This may have been out of fear, or loyalty to Henry. While it's impossible to know how many people disagreed privately, only a few courageous and principled individuals decided to make a stand. Awaiting them was the full horror of Tudor law enforcement. The three most important opponents are shown below.

I oppose the Reformation because I believe Protestantism threatens the souls of English people. I cannot publically support Henry's split with Rome, or his divorce.

Thomas More

I oppose the Reformation because I have had visions from God. He has told me he approves of mass and other Catholic practises. If the king divorces his Catholic wife, he will die a villain's death.

Elizabeth Barton

I oppose the Reformation because I believe that Catherine of Aragon is Henry's lawful wedded wife. I also oppose the split with Rome because the powers used by the pope were given by God. By claiming them as his own, Henry is committing a mortal sin.

John Fisher

Figure 3.3 The three main figures opposing the Reformation.

Elizabeth Barton, the Nun of Kent

In a superstitious age, people who claimed they had supernatural gifts were often taken very seriously. In 1525, Elizabeth Barton, an unknown but very ill 16-year-old, made the sensational claim that the Virgin Mary had appeared to her in a vision and miraculously cured her.

She entered a convent in Canterbury, where her visions and reputation continued to develop. Thousands flocked to see her, including the nobility and gentry. According to the future archbishop, Thomas Cranmer, in her visions:

- she would enter a trance
- her face became disfigured
- she spoke without moving her lips
- her voice took on a terrifying tone when describing hell.

From 1527, Elizabeth's visions became more problematic for Henry VIII. She started attacking Henry's plans to divorce Catherine of Aragon, as well as Protestant ideas in general. She spoke about the need to burn English translations of the Bible and to remain loyal to the pope. She said that God approved of pilgrimages and the practise of mass. In a face-to-face meeting with the king in 1532, she warned him that, if he married Anne Boleyn, he would die a villain's death within a month.

It is impossible to know if Elizabeth was a fraud or genuinely believed in her prophesies. It is probable, though, that she was being exploited by a small group of clergymen who opposed the king's policies. The nun's spiritual adviser, a monk called Dr Edward Bocking, was among these people. In 1533, he published a collection of her prophecies called the *Nun's Book*. He was also making links with the leading opponents of Henry's reforms, including Bishop Fisher and Thomas More.

In July 1533, Henry ordered Cromwell to act. The visions were not only embarrassing for Henry, but also dangerous. They had the potential to inspire people to resist his religious reforms. The timeline shows what happened next.

Timeline
The death of Elizabeth Barton

July 1533 Elizabeth Barton is arrested, taken to the Tower of London and interrogated

All 700 copies of the *Nun's Book* are seized and destroyed. Not a single copy survives

23 November 1533 Elizabeth is publicly humiliated at St Paul's Cross in London, where she is forced to confess to lying about her visions

21 April 1534 Elizabeth is executed for treason, along with Edward Bocking.

The timing of the execution was calculated. On the same day, Londoners were required to take the Oath of Succession

John Fisher

John Fisher provided a stronger challenge to Henry's reforms than Elizabeth Barton. Appointed Bishop of Rochester in 1504, he developed a European-wide reputation as a scholar. He tutored Henry as a young prince, and then supported him throughout his early reign.

However, Fisher found it impossible to support Henry after 1527. He believed that Catherine of Aragon was Henry's lawful wedded wife and became outspoken against the king's efforts to secure a divorce. He also opposed Henry's move to split with Rome because he believed the powers used by the pope were given by God. By claiming them as his own, Henry was committing a mortal sin.

While other bishops agreed with Fisher privately, they supported Henry publicly. Despite pressure from other members of the clergy and threats from the king's men, Fisher would not change his mind.

Unsurprisingly, Henry grew to hate Fisher, but could not do anything to stop him, as he had not broken any laws. However, when Elizabeth Barton was arrested in 1533, Fisher's links with her meant that he could be charged with treason. Perhaps because of his high status, he escaped much more lightly than her, with a fine of £300, and continued to oppose Henry's religious reforms.

In fact, Fisher grew more determined, secretly appealing to Charles V to invade England – though no reply was ever received. In April 1534, Henry demanded that Fisher take the Oath of Succession. When he refused, unable to bring himself to acknowledge Anne Boleyn as the true queen, he was sent to the Tower of London.

In May 1535, the pope announced that Fisher was to be made a Cardinal. While the pope hoped this would encourage leniency on Henry's part, it instead made the king determined to prove who was in control. Fisher was executed for treason in June 1535. He was the only bishop to be killed for opposing tne Royal Supremacy.

The significance of opposition from Thomas More

Two weeks after Fisher's death, Sir Thomas More was also executed. Source A shows More eight years earlier: intelligent, calm, determined and comfortable with power. This was a man who had built a reputation as one of Europe's leading scholars. His greatest work was the novel *Utopia*. Published in 1516, it described a perfect society, complete with a six-hour working day, a national health service, education, religious toleration and rights for women.

However, More was a devout Catholic – and his belief in religious toleration only stretched so far.

In 1527, More wrote that Martin Luther and his followers were criminals who 'bespatter the most holy image of Christ crucified with the most foul excrement of their bodies'. He believed Protestantism threatened the souls of English people. More was appointed Lord Chancellor in 1529, following the fall of Wolsey. He banned all Protestant books and personally hunted out and interrogated suspected heretics. During his Chancellorship, six people were burnt for their Protestant beliefs.

By 1532, More could no longer work for Henry, as his Catholic principles went against Henry's wish to divorce Catherine of Aragon and break from Rome. However, More was a loyal subject and did not wish to oppose the king; so he resigned the chancellorship, claiming ill health.

Source A

Thomas More by Hans Holbein, painted in 1527.

He planned to retire from public life and remain silent about Henry's divorce and his break from Rome; but unfortunately for More, Henry would not allow this. The king believed that those who were not with him were against him. Because More wouldn't offer his public support Henry saw him as a dangerous enemy to be hounded.

In April 1534, More, most likely on Henry's urging, was asked to take the Oath of Succession. When he refused, he was sent to the Tower of London. While More was not prepared to betray his principles, he also had no wish to die, and so placed his hopes on silence. Over his yearlong imprisonment, More repeatedly refused to explain why he would not take the Oath. He knew that if he revealed his real reason, and denied Henry as the legitimate head of the Church, he would be committing treason.

However, during his trial in July 1535, evidence was produced showing that he had spoken his true feelings about Henry and the break with Rome. This evidence was probably made up, but it was enough for More to be executed under the new Treason Act.

The fate of Thomas More can be seen as significant for four main reasons.

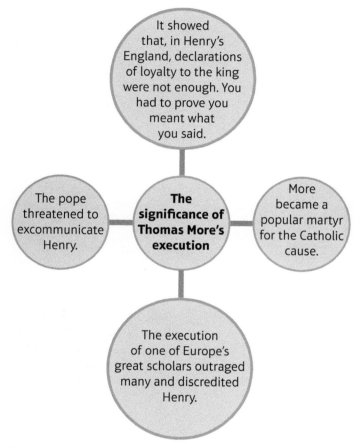

Figure 3.4 The significance of Thomas More's execution.

Interpretation 1

In this extract, Tracy Borman, a historian specialising in Thomas Cromwell, was interviewed by *The Telegraph* in January 2015 about her views on More and Cromwell.

Historians often say of the two of them, you can't like both. You have to choose one or the other – More or Cromwell – and More has been ahead in the PR game from the start. You could even say that his execution, for a point of principle, was a masterstroke, and gave him an unassailable lead for centuries… Yet they were both lawyers, both clever, both good at debating and even had a grudging respect for each other.

The impact of the Reformation on the English Church

The 1534 Act of Supremacy changed the structure of the Church by cutting links with Rome and establishing the king as its new leader. The pope, however, had always been a remote and distant figure, so for most people this change of leadership had no impact on the way they worshipped God.

From 1534–40, however, a more significant struggle began. It was fought between religious reformers and conservative Catholics, each group trying to persuade Henry VIII to change the English Church to reflect their views.

Cromwell and Thomas Cranmer, the Archbishop of Canterbury, believed that what the Church preached should be based solely on the teachings of the Bible. This was a very Protestant way of thinking. However, to be openly Protestant in England at this time was highly dangerous. Despite splitting with Rome, Henry was still a Catholic and opposed many aspects of Protestantism. A priest, John Frith, discovered this when, in 1533, he was burned at the stake for denying transubstantiation. Therefore, supporters of religious reform had to be extremely cautious in the way they pushed for change.

Opposing Cromwell and Cranmer were powerful figures such as Thomas Howard, the Duke of Norfolk, and Stephen Gardiner, Bishop of Winchester. As loyal Catholics, they firmly believed in traditional Catholic rules. However, they had to be cautious, too. To be seen as a supporter of the pope and opposed to the Royal Supremacy was a traitorous act, punishable by death.

Although this was a complex argument, the outcome did not lead to any radical transformation in the English Church up to 1540.

The influence of Cromwell

For a time, Henry, despite his Catholic outlook, showed some sympathy to reformist ideas. The table opposite shows how Cromwell was able to make changes in slow, gradual steps.

Event	Description	Significance
July 1536 **Act of Ten Articles issued**	People should only believe three of the seven sacraments; baptism, the Eucharist and penance.	This was the first attempt to set out the beliefs of Henry's new church. It represented a partial move towards Protestantism by reducing the sacraments.
August 1536 **The first set of Royal Injunctions issued to the clergy by Cromwell**	The clergy were ordered to speak in favour of the Royal Supremacy and Ten Articles. Priests were ordered to discourage pilgrimages and the number of Holy Days dedicated to saints was reduced.	This was an attempt to ensure all the clergy delivered the same message. Many Catholic practices seen as superstitious were attacked.
July 1537 **Bishops Book published**	The four sacraments ignored by the Ten Articles were declared valid, although of lesser value. It stated the main duty of a priest was preaching.	This was a second major attempt to outline what the Church believed. The re-inclusion of the four sacraments was a slight set-back for reformers. Overall, it was a further move towards Protestantism: it deliberately lessened the importance of some core Catholic beliefs which Protestants believed had no value.
September 1538 **The second set of Royal Injunctions issued to the clergy by Cromwell**	An English translation of the Bible was to be placed in all churches within two years. Priests were to actively discourage pilgrimages, and religious images, statues and relics were to be removed from churches.	This was far more detailed than the set of instructions issued to the clergy in 1536. An English Bible was a major victory for religious reformers who wanted the Bible to be read by ordinary people. It was a direct attack on how Catholics worshipped and led to the disappearance of shrines, statues and relics from Churches. For example, St Thomas Becket's Shrine, one of the most famous pilgrimage sites in Europe, was destroyed.

The work of Cranmer

Despite being the Church's most senior member of the clergy, Archbishop Cranmer acted as the supporting figure to Cromwell. He helped draft the Ten Articles and Bishops Book, and assisted in arguing for a Bible in English. Unlike Cromwell, Cranmer was no politician. He was a man of little ambition and, up until his mid-forties, was happy living in obscurity. His appointment as Archbishop of Canterbury in 1533 took everyone by surprise. He had attracted Henry's attention by supporting his divorce.

As the king's servant, Cranmer was prepared to be flexible in his beliefs in order to please his master. This even included letting Protestants be burnt to death, even though they shared similar beliefs to him.

Henry VIII and a return to Catholicism

By the end of the decade, Henry decided that religious reform had gone too far. In 1538, he decided to return to traditional Catholic values. To prove this, he had the priest John Lambert repeatedly plunged into flames for denying transubstantiation. Henry looked on, robed in white to show the purity of his Catholic faith.

In 1539, Henry published the **Six Articles**, which were a clear statement of Catholic doctrine. It confirmed transubstantiation and purgatory, as well as the special role of priests by stating they had to remain celibate*. Cranmer, who was married, sent his wife and children abroad for safety. Failure to agree to the Six Articles could lead to imprisonment, confiscation of property, or even death.

Reformist ideas made only slow progress by 1540. Given Henry's own opposition to Protestantism, this should not be surprising. However, some traditional Catholic practices were gradually stopped, such as pilgrimages, Saints Days and the worshiping of relics and images. A major objective of the religious reformers had also been achieved with the introduction of the Bible in English. They believed that once ordinary people could read the Word of God, further reform would become inevitable. Despite this hope for the future, there were no such reforms after 1540 under Henry VIII.

Key term

Celibate*

Being unmarried or not involved in sexual relationships.

Exam-style question, Section B

'In the years 1534–40 the English Church changed very little'. How far do you agree? Explain your answer.

You may use the following in your answer:

- The Act of Supremacy (1534)
- The Six Articles (1539).

You **must** also use information of your own.　　**16 marks**

Exam tip

To do well in this question you must provide points for and against this statement. It must also be well organised and written in clear paragraphs. Each paragraph should explain a distinct point.

Source B

The front cover of the Great Bible, printed in 1539. It was the first official translation of the Bible in English and represented a significant victory for religious reformers. It also displays Henry's new religious order. Christ looks down directly on Henry, who is seen handing this new Bible to Archbishop Cranmer on his right and Cromwell on his left. The pope is notably absent. Nine thousand copies of the Great Bible were printed between 1539 and 1541.

Summary

- Henry VIII's decision to divorce Catherine of Aragon and then make himself head of the Church was highly controversial and resented by many.
- The number of people who actively resisted was small. The most high profile opponents from the church were Elizabeth Barton and John Fisher. Thomas More was the leading opponent from within Henry's government.
- In the years 1534–40, the English Church went through further reform.
- The English Church was pushed toward a more Protestant direction by introducing the English Bible.
- Superstitious practices, such as praying to relics, statues and shrines, were banned.
- Many elements of the Catholic Church service remained, including the traditional mass.

Checkpoint

Strengthen

S1 Briefly describe the different ways in which Barton, Fisher and More opposed Henry's religious changes.

S2 Note down three religious changes that ordinary people would have noticed by 1540.

Challenge

C1 More's last words were 'The King's good servant, but God's first'. What do you think he meant by this?

C2 Was the opposition to the break with Rome a serious threat to Henry? Why?

C3 Was Henry's new church best described as 'Catholicism without the pope'? Explain your answer.

How confident do you feel about your answers to these questions? If you are not sure, it might help to discuss your ideas with other students.

Learning outcomes

- Understand the main reasons for Henry VIII's decision to close the monasteries.
- Understand that the closure of the monasteries had both negative and positive impacts for different people.

At the start of Henry's reign, England was a land of abbeys and monasteries. Across the country, there were over 800 religious houses served by 10,000 monks and nuns. The religious, welfare and educational roles of the monasteries placed them at the heart of many communities.

In November 1534, Henry became head of the English Church as a result of the Act of Supremacy and the monasteries fell under his direct power. From 1536, he began their destruction. By 1540, not a single one remained. One of the largest abbeys to close is shown in Source A.

Timeline

The dissolution of the monasteries

1535 A survey into Church wealth is carried out (*Valor Ecclesiasticus*)

Cromwell investigates the moral state of the monasteries

1538-40 Voluntary dissolution of the remaining larger monasteries

March 1536 Parliament passes the first Act of Dissolution of the Monasteries

October–December 1536 Pilgrimage of Grace uprising against the closure of the monasteries

1539 The second Act for the Dissolution of the Monasteries is passed

Source A

A photograph of the ruins of Glastonbury Abbey today.

The role of religious houses in local communities

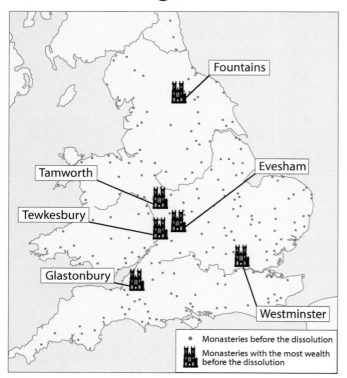

Figure 3.5 Monasteries of England and Wales before the dissolution.

For England's nearly 8,000 monks and 2,000 nuns, the focus of their day was **religious contemplation** – this meant they spent their time thinking about ways to better serve God. It was a never-ending cycle. Prayers and worship began at 2 a.m., with the first of eight daily services. In order to make sure there were no distractions from their worship of God, all monks and nuns were expected to be poor, chaste and obedient. As a result of this strict lifestyle and unique religious role, monks and nuns generally enjoyed a powerful reputation and were treated with great respect.

However, the monasteries were not just significant because of prayer. Collectively, the monasteries owned around one-third of all the lands in England. This meant that heads of houses were, in effect, managing directors of big business, acting as landlords, estate managers and controlling large budgets. The top 20 houses had incomes of over £1,000 per year, which made them as wealthy as leading nobles. In addition, heads of houses played a role in administering local justice, while 30 sat in the House of Lords and helped advise the king.

The children of the wealthy were often educated by monks and nuns.

Travellers on long journeys could use the network of religious houses as safe places to stay.

The heads of the most important religious houses helped advise the king.

Poor people could go to their local monasteries to receive food and help.

Large areas of the countryside were owned by monasteries.

The sick were often treated in hospitals set up by the monasteries.

Monks and nuns produced beautiful works of art such as illuminated manuscripts.

Monks and nuns would pray for the souls of the dead.

Figure 3.6 The role of monasteries in England.

Monasteries were also places of shelter and safety for travellers in an age when journeys were difficult and dangerous. They were supporters of the arts, centres of education for the wealthy, and also charitable institutions – running hospitals for the sick and providing food for the poor. Therefore, monks and nuns were a familiar and accepted part of local life and were found in towns, as well as the countryside.

Extend your knowledge

Monasteries

The term 'monasteries' was not commonly used in Tudor times. Larger, mainly rural institutions tended to be called **abbeys**; medium sized houses were **priories** or **nunneries**; and the smaller houses, principally based in towns, were **friaries**.

Reasons for the dissolutions

Many different motives influenced Henry's decision to close the monasteries, although some were more important than others. The dissolution was chiefly about Henry's need for money. It was a 'smash and grab' operation.

Cromwell's commission of 1535

Although Henry's main reason for closing the monasteries was financial, the public reason was the spiritual and moral decay of the monasteries. As Source B shows, the introduction to the 1536 Act of Dissolution painted a damming picture of the smaller religious houses.

Source B

From the Act of Dissolution of the Monasteries in 1536 – dissolving monasteries with an income of less than £200 a year.

… sin, vicious, carnal and abominable living is being daily used and committed among the small abbeys, priories and other religious houses. The governors of such religious houses spoil, destroy, consume and utterly waste their properties to the high displeasure of almighty God. And although many continual visitations have been made for an honest and charitable reformation, yet their vicious living shamelessly increases, so that unless such small houses are utterly suppressed there can be no reform of these matters.

A series of official inspections were carried out in 1535 by six of Cromwell's servants, including Richard Layton and Thomas Legh. These **visitations**, as they were called, had been ordered by Cromwell, who was responsible for the day-to-day control of the Church.

The findings, listed in a document called the *Compendium Compertorum*, were bleak. They claimed that hundreds of monks had admitted to taking part in homosexual practices, often with young boys; and others had confessed to keeping mistresses. They also found many cases of nuns bearing children. There were also reports that Abbot Hexham of Whitby allegedly worked in league with French pirates!

All these things went against the strict moral code of the Church. Given the seriousness of the charges, it was not hard to justify the dissolution of smaller monasteries.

Although generally accepted at the time, the visitations do not provide reliable and accurate evidence.

- The inspections were not thorough, with only a few hours being spent in each house. Layton and Legh apparently visited over 120 houses in under 70 days.
- Layton and Legh used bullying tactics when questioning monks and nuns.
- Little effort was made to present a balanced picture, with most focus being on the negatives, and evidence being exaggerated or changed.
- Historians have since been able to show the inaccuracy of the visitations' most sensational claims. For example, of the 181 claims of homosexual practices, only 12 appear to be true.

Also, the public were not against the monasteries, which would have been expected had the claims been true.

It is now generally agreed that, while there were certainly some corrupt monasteries, there were also some good ones. For example, Whalley Abbey in Lancashire distributed 22% of its income to charity, well above the average figure of 2–3%.

Most monasteries, though, were in the middle of this 'good' and 'bad' spectrum; and they do not appear to have been any more corrupt than the wider Church.

Why would Cromwell's servants report that the monasteries were corrupt if they were not? Legh and Layton were ambitious men and knew that the only way to get ahead was to give their master, Cromwell, exactly what he wanted. In this case, it was to provide him with proof that would close the monasteries.

Henry, and therefore Cromwell, wanted the monasteries gone. The decision had already been made. Therefore, it is necessary to look elsewhere for the true causes of the dissolution.

New religious ideas

The dissolution partly reflected the growing belief among religious reformers that monasteries were not useful. One leading opponent of the monasteries, Erasmus, described monks as 'counterfeit holy and idle beggars'. The primary role of monks and nuns was to pray for the souls of the dead, and ordinary people were encouraged to give donations so this could be carried out. To Protestants, this was wrong. Protestants believed that the only way people would get to heaven was by individually praying to God.

These new religious ideas certainly influenced Cromwell, who was the single most important figure in the dissolution apart from Henry. However, Henry, showed his support for the traditional role of monasteries by re-founding two of them in 1537; Bisham Abbey and the nunnery of Stixwold. Their purpose was to provide frequent prayers for him, his wife Jane Seymour, and their heirs and ancestors. This makes it seem doubtful that Henry ordered the dissolution because he truly believed the ideas of the religious reformers.

Loyalty

However, Henry did have doubts about the loyalty of the monasteries. While the 1534 Act of Supremacy had placed him in charge of the English Church, many religious houses had strong links with Rome and the pope. There was fierce resistance from some monks after the split from Rome, which highlights how strong the bonds with the pope were.

In truth, Henry had little to worry about. Nearly every monk and nun ended up swearing an oath accepting the Act of Succession. Eighteen monks resisted, and they were executed as a warning. However, the issue of loyalty seems to have played on Henry's mind. He could not tolerate the thought of monks and nuns owing their loyalty to someone else.

Money

Henry's main motivation was financial – he wanted more money, and monasteries were wealthy institutions. Henry discovered this for himself when he commissioned a survey into their wealth, known as the *Valor Ecclesiasticus*. This literally meant 'the value of the Church.' It revealed that the monasteries owned one-third of English land and had a total income of £160,000 a year, or three times the income of royal estates. For Henry, the chance to lay his hands on this wealth was not only desirable, it was essential.

- The money would finance Henry's wars.
- People were worried that Catholics would invade England. Extra money could help pay to protect England.
- Henry would no longer need to rely on parliament to grant him taxation. The taxpayers' revolt following Wolsey's 1525 Amicable Grant had shown that this was a problematic source of taxation (see page 19).
- Any land taken from the monasteries could be given as gifts as a way of buying support from the gentry and nobility.

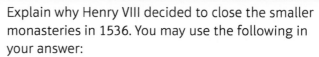

Exam-style question, Section B

Explain why Henry VIII decided to close the smaller monasteries in 1536. You may use the following in your answer:

- the *Valor Ecclesiasticus*
- Cromwell's commissions.

You **must** also use information of your own. **12 marks**

Exam tip

Remember that you cannot get the highest marks if you do not go beyond the stimulus points listed. A good additional factor to talk about for this question would be Henry's concern over the loyalty of the monks and nuns.

The process of dissolution

England's 800 monasteries were destroyed in two stages. Based on the damning findings of Cromwell's servants, parliament passed the **first Act of Dissolution** in March 1536, closing 300 smaller monasteries with an income of less than £200 a year. Royal commissioners were then appointed to each county to oversee the closures.

It is uncertain whether, at this stage, Henry had a grand plan for closing all the monasteries. The first Act of Dissolution allowed 67 smaller monasteries, judged to be carrying out their spiritual work effectively, to stay open.

However, towards the end of 1537, the decision was taken to close the larger monasteries, too. This is partly because some had supported the rebels in the Pilgrimage of Grace (see pages 85–90), but mainly because of their wealth.

In order to avoid a rebellion against Henry, no sweeping second dissolution law was passed. Instead, each monastery was individually targeted by Cromwell's servants from 1538 in another series of visitations. The abbots and abbesses were 'invited' to voluntarily surrender their houses to the king as a free gift. Most realised that they could not say no. The offer of a generous pension may have also helped. Those that did not agree were later forced to resign by royal command and were replaced by people more willing to agree to the king's wishes. In 1539, parliament passed a second Act of Dissolution confirming the 'voluntary' surrenders. By 1540, the process had been completed and not a single monastery remained.

The impact of the dissolutions: winners and losers

Deciding exactly where the balance lies between winners and losers is one of the dissolution's central questions. It involves weighing conflicting evidence and making difficult judgements.

Winners	Losers
Religious reformers who opposed the monasteries	Monks and nuns who lost their way of life
Henry VIII who became richer than ever	Catholics who valued the prayers said by monks and nuns
Gentry and nobles who bought monastic estates	The poor and sick who depended on the monasteries
	Some tenant farmers who saw rents rise after the dissolution

The Winners
Religious and financial winners
While a lot of the evidence suggests the impact of the dissolution was mixed, there were certainly outright winners. For Protestants, the closure of the monasteries removed a powerful symbol of Roman Catholicism. For the Crown, it brought huge financial gain.

Over time, Henry sold most of the monastic land. This gave members of the nobility the opportunity to buy land previously owned by the monasteries.

A lot of estates were also bought by those who ordinarily would have remained landless, including wealthy merchants and lawyers.

The Losers
Human cost
The dissolution involved a period of hard readjustment for many monks and nuns. The monasteries were far more than just places of work. Each monastery was also a home – offering accommodation, food and companionship. Their closure must have been bewildering and frightening for those who lived, worked and worshipped in them.

Careful research has been carried out into the fate of monks and nuns after the dissolution. The heads of houses were granted a relatively generous pension, while ordinary monks and nuns were given a one-off payment of 20 to 30 shillings. It is estimated that about 6,500 out of 8,000 monks managed to secure alternative paid employment in the Church, and with it a comfortable enough living. However, a significant number were left in hardship. There are many contemporary stories of monks becoming beggars. England's 2,000 nuns suffered the most. They were not allowed to either marry or work in churches. Life must have been very tough.

Monks and nuns were not the only ones badly affected. The dissolution has been suggested as a reason for Tudor England's rising levels of poverty. This is partly because of the loss of the monasteries charitable work. In addition, some of the landlords who replaced the monks were ruthless in pursuit of profit. They raised rents or threw tenants off the land to graze sheep instead.

Cultural impact

Source C

An extract from a lengthy speech by Robert Aske, leader of the Pilgrimage of Grace, spoken while awaiting execution in 1537.

The Abbeys were one of the beauties of this realm.

As Source C shows, the destruction of the monastic buildings can also be seen as an act of **cultural vandalism**. The majestic remains of abbeys, such as Glastonbury and Fountains in Yorkshire, suggest the quality of architecture which was lost. In addition, many of the treasures of the monasteries, such as the libraries, art, stained glass windows and furnishings, were sold off or destroyed. Henry's decision to install the church windows of Rewley Abbey, near Oxford, in his bowling alley at Hampton Court seems particularly insensitive.

However many of the monastic buildings which were destroyed were run down anyway; and others managed to survive. Tewkesbury Abbey was bought by locals and turned into a parish church. Others became cathedrals, such as Bristol and Westminster. Henry also made an attempt to compensate for the loss of the monasteries' role in education. New cathedral grammar schools were set up in towns such as Canterbury, Carlisle, Ely and Bristol; while two colleges were established in Oxford and Cambridge: Christ Church and Trinity College.

Activity ?

1 In small groups, decide where the following should be placed on a scale of 1 to 10 – with 1 being clear losers as a result of the Dissolution of the monasteries, and 10 being clear winners:

   a Henry VIII

   b Monks

   c Nuns

   d The nobility

   e Protestants

   f Local communities

   g Catholics

   h Thomas Cromwell.

2 Write a short paragraph explaining your decision.

Summary

- The main purpose of England's 800 monasteries before the Reformation was to pray for the souls of the dead. They also carried out charitable, artistic and educational work.

- As a result of the Act of Supremacy, Henry became head of the monasteries. Cromwell, as Vicegerent, was in charge of overseeing their day-to-day running.

- Between 1536–40, all of England's monasteries were closed down. The first and second Dissolution Acts provided the legal basis for this.

- Henry VIII was primarily concerned about gaining the wealth of the monasteries. The scale of this had been revealed by the *Valor Ecclesiasticus*.

- Dissolution impacted those who relied on monasteries for charity. Nuns also suffered but most monks found new employment. The winners were Henry VIII, religious reformers, and those able to buy monastic estates.

Checkpoint

Strengthen

S1 Describe the range of work carried out by monasteries.

S2 Describe the steps taken by Cromwell to investigate the monasteries in 1535.

Challenge

C1 Do the reports of corruption and immorality in the monasteries provide a full explanation for their closure?

C2 What were the main differences between the first and second Acts of Dissolution?

C3 Overall, do you think that there were more winners than losers as a result of the dissolution of the monasteries?

In March 1536, parliament changed England for ever by passing the first Dissolution Act. By the summer of 1536, royal commissioners were at work overseeing the closure of the monasteries and seizing their valuables. Henry and Cromwell did not know how local people would react to this assault on centuries of tradition – but they soon found out.

Although most of England remained quiet, by the autumn of 1536 a major rebellion had developed in the North. This part of England was traditionally very Catholic. Discontent began in Lincolnshire but soon spread to Yorkshire. Here, a huge army of 40,000 rebels gathered and started heading south under the leadership of a one-eyed lawyer named **Robert Aske**. Henry VIII's throne seemed in danger.

Reasons for the uprising

With autumn proving unusually wet, and winter on the horizon, what pushed the people of the North to leave their homes and challenge the Crown? As Figure 3.7 shows, religious, political, social and economic factors all played a role. Above all, the Northerners wanted to defend their Roman Catholic faith. The importance of religion as a motivating factor is shown by the decision to call the rebellion 'the Pilgrimage of Grace'.

Religious Factors

- The North was mainly Catholic, and many believed their faith was under threat.
- The dissolution of the smaller monasteries was seen as an unforgivable attack on religion.
- The work of monks and nuns was important for the whole community.
- The dissolution led to fears that the parish churches would be the next target.

Social Factors

The monasteries provided:

- healing for the sick
- help for the poor
- refuge for travellers.

The fact that this was all under threat through the dissolution angered many.

Economic Factors

- The 1534 Subsidy Act was still being collected in 1536. This was usually only raised in wartime. As England was at peace, it was deeply resented.
- Poor harvests in 1535 and 1536 made times even harder.
- Commoners had complaints about rising rents and enclosure of common land.
- Gentry and nobility were opposed to the 1536 **Statute of Uses**, a tax on landed inheritances.

Political Factors

- The northern nobility felt that Henry's court was too much under the influence of Cromwell.
- They disliked Cromwell for his low birth and reformist religious views.
- They hoped the uprising would increase their power in court and weaken Cromwell's.

Figure 3.7 The main reasons for the Pilgrimage of Grace.

An image of the badge worn by those on the Pilgrimage of Grace, showing the five wounds of Christ.

The participants viewed themselves not as rebels, but as Christ's soldiers. They wore badges depicting the five wounds Christ had received on the cross (see Source A) and swore a religious oath (shown in Source B). They marched singing hymns and carrying religious banners, including the velvet, gold and silk banner of St Cuthbert, brought down from Durham Cathedral. In the areas they occupied, the Pilgrims restored 16 religious houses, such as the nunnery of St Clement's in York and Sawley Abbey on the banks of the River Ribble.

Key events of the uprising
Rebellion in Lincolnshire

Trouble first broke out in Lincolnshire. Since the summer, it had been a county under pressure. Three government commissions were at work: the first dissolving the smaller monasteries, the second collecting taxation, and the third investigating the quality of the clergy. Wild rumours also circulated that many parish churches were going to be closed. On 2 October, the people of Lincolnshire finally snapped. Led by a local shoe maker, **Nicholas Melton**, who gave himself the title Captain Cobbler, 3,000 commoners rose up.

By the 4 October, leadership of the uprising had passed to the gentry. This stopped it from being a mob and turned it into a more focused political demonstration. However, passions were still hard to contain. On the 4 October, Dr Raynes, the hated chancellor of the Bishop of Lincoln, was murdered by a frenzied mob in Horncastle. He had been conducting the enquiry into the fitness of the clergy. On 7 October, at least 10,000 rebels marched on the county town of Lincoln. A set of Articles was drawn up and sent to London. These cited, among other grievances, the Dissolution of the monasteries and high taxes. The king, though, was in no mood to listen.

- Henry sent the rebels a message threatening extreme punishment if they did not stop their rebellion, including the destruction of all their property. It reached them on 10 October.
- Henry raised and dispatched a force of around 3,000 men, under **Charles Brandon, the Duke of Suffolk**.

To the commoners' fury, this was enough to make the gentry in charge of the rebellion back down. The gentry realised that any further resistance would be treason, and withdrew their support, asking for a royal pardon. With their natural leaders gone, the remainder of the rebels began dispersing. By the 11 October, the Lincolnshire rebellion was over.

An extract from the Pilgrims' oath taken in October, 1536.

And that ye shall not enter into our said Pilgrimage for no particular profit to yourself, nor to do any displeasure to any private person... but in your hearts put away fear and dread, and take afore you the Cross of Christ, and in your hearts His faith...

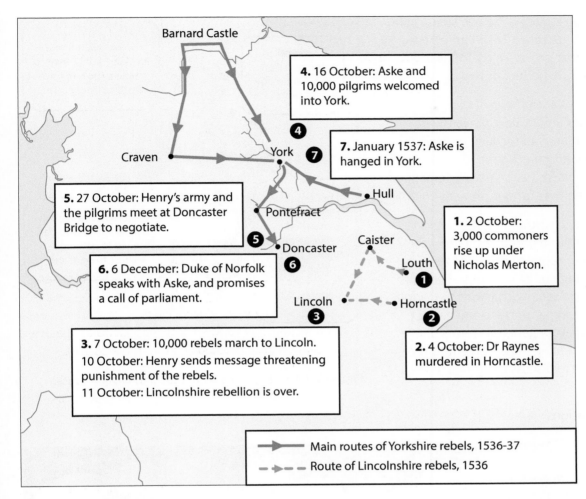

4. 16 October: Aske and 10,000 pilgrims welcomed into York.

7. January 1537: Aske is hanged in York.

5. 27 October: Henry's army and the pilgrims meet at Doncaster Bridge to negotiate.

1. 2 October: 3,000 commoners rise up under Nicholas Merton.

6. 6 December: Duke of Norfolk speaks with Aske, and promises a call of parliament.

3. 7 October: 10,000 rebels march to Lincoln.
10 October: Henry sends message threatening punishment of the rebels.
11 October: Lincolnshire rebellion is over.

2. 4 October: Dr Raynes murdered in Horncastle.

→ Main routes of Yorkshire rebels, 1536-37
--→ Route of Lincolnshire rebels, 1536

Figure 3.8 The Pilgrimage of Grace.

The Yorkshire Rebellion

From early October 1536, a larger, more serious uprising started in Yorkshire. It had better leadership than the Lincolnshire revolt. In a matter of three weeks, 40,000 men had formed into nine well-armed hosts (or armies). Each one was led by a respected member of the community, from the gentry or nobility. These leaders, known as **captains**, were in close contact with each other and met regularly during the uprising to discuss strategy. The most important army was led by a lawyer in his late thirties, **Robert Aske**. Aske soon emerged as the overall leader of the movement, and was key in determining the rebel strategy.

In staging their show of force, the Pilgrims enjoyed early success and took over much of the country north of the River Don. This included key strategic locations. York, the most important city in the North, welcomed

Aske and his army of 10,000 Pilgrims on 16 October. In return, Aske ensured there was no looting and all goods used were paid for. On 19 October, the important town of Hull surrendered after a five day siege. On 21 October, Pontefract Castle, known as 'the gateway to the North' also fell. The castle's garrison under **Lord Darcy** only put up half-hearted resistance, and he then joined the rebel cause. As a member of the nobility, Darcy's support was a boost for the Pilgrims. Only a few isolated pockets held out including Skipton Castle, Carlisle and Newcastle.

The revolt caught Henry by surprise, but when its scale became clear, he mustered a new army and gave its command to **Thomas Howard, Duke of Norfolk**. As shown in Figure 3.10, Norfolk realised that the Pilgrims could not be defeated in battle. Despite his orders to crush the revolt, he chose to negotiate instead.

As this fitted Aske's overall strategy, the two sides met on Doncaster Bridge on 27 October. The Pilgrim's used the occasion to display their power. Thirty thousand rebels lined the river bank, in perfect order.

The result of this meeting was that two of the Pilgrim leaders, **Sir Ralph Ellerker** and **Robert Bowes**, were allowed to carry their demands to the king himself. Little, though, was achieved from this meeting. Henry refused to discuss terms himself and instead demanded ten ringleaders be handed over for punishment.

However, Henry did agree to further negotiations through the Duke of Norfolk. In preparation for these, Aske and the other Pilgrim captains compiled the **Pontefract Articles**, setting out 24 demands. The king also made preparations. He sent instructions to Norfolk, ordering him to secure a long term truce and giving him the power to offer the very generous terms of a full pardon, and the summoning of parliament to the North of England in order to discuss the terms of the Pontefract Articles.

However, Henry's negotiations were a bluff.

Figure 3.9 Aske as the leader of the Pilgrimage of Grace.

Figure 3.10 Pilgrim leaders and the Duke of Norfolk negotiate on Doncaster Bridge on 27 October, 1536.

Source C

Extracts from the Pontefract Articles, written by the Pilgrim leader, Robert Aske, 2–4 December 1536.

1. *The first touching our faith. To have the heresies of Luther... to be annulled and destroyed.*

2. *The second to have the supreme head of the Church ... to be restored unto the see of Rome as before it was accustomed to be...*

3. *We humbly beseech our most dread sovereign lord that the lady Mary may be made legitimate...*

4. *To have the abbeys suppressed to be restored to their houses, lands, and goods.*

Henry's bluff

On 6 December, 40 Pilgrim representatives, led by Aske, met the Duke of Norfolk in Doncaster. After long discussions, they accepted the king's offer of a pardon and a parliament. They also secured a promise that no further monasteries would be closed until the new parliament had met.

Unsurprisingly, Aske thought that he had won and felt confident enough to recommend the terms to his fellow Pilgrims. He even tore off the badge of the Five Wounds, reportedly saying 'We will all wear no badge nor sign but the badge of our sovereign lord'. Many expressed concern over whether Henry could be trusted and only reluctantly accepted the deal. Nevertheless, Aske took the decision to disband the huge Pilgrim Army.

It became clear very quickly that the real victor in the negotiations was Henry.

- Norfolk had been able to avoid any serious discussion on the Pontefract Articles by arguing that this could be carried out by parliament.
- He had avoided committing himself as to when and where the parliament should be held.
- The terms of the agreement had not been written down.
- Henry had no intention of keeping to the agreement anyway. He believed that promises made to rebels could be broken, because they were traitors.
- He had removed the immediate threat of a rebel army marching south, and now had time to prepare his revenge.

Crushing the revolt

By January 1537, the lack of news on the promised parliament was causing growing concern among the Pilgrims. Because of this, two small, unco-ordinated uprisings took place, one aimed at capturing Hull, the other Carlisle. While both quickly fizzled out, they provided Henry with the excuse he needed to punish the Pilgrims. He ordered Norfolk to round up the Pilgrim ringleaders and execute them. The final death toll stood at 178, including Aske himself. He was hanged in York because Henry wanted his execution carried out in the place most associated with the Pilgrimage of Grace.

The table below shows the roles played by Robert Aske and Thomas Howard in the Pilgrimage of Grace.

Robert Aske	Thomas Howard, The Duke of Norfolk
Inspirational rebel leader	Placed in charge of suppressing the revolt by Henry VIII
Ensured the rebel army remained well-behaved	Led a Royal Army to the North of England.
Ruled out fighting the King's Army	Decided not to use force against the rebel army
Set out the rebel demands in the 'Pontefract Articles'	Met the rebels twice to discuss their demands
Negotiated with the king's representative, the Duke of Norfolk	Negotiated the key deal which saw the rebels disband their army
Decided to trust Henry VIII and accept his promises	Executed the leading rebels
Paid for this with his life	

Reasons for the revolt's failure and its significance

The rebellion had been a failure, achieving none of its grand aims. This was principally because of Aske's misplaced faith in the king. He believed that Henry would be willing to negotiate and could be trusted. However, Aske had failed to appreciate the nature of Henry's kingship. To be seen giving into the rebels would have fatally weakened his status as ruler.

It would also have represented the complete surrender of the whole of his political and religious policy.

Why, then, did Aske trust the king? Aske could be seen as naïve, but this would be unfair judgement.

- Aske was a sharp minded, educated lawyer.
- Henry gave no reason for Aske to be distrustful. He was even invited to spend Christmas in Henry's court, where he was treated with considerable respect.

Although a failure, the Pilgrimage of Grace was still historically significant and deserves to be remembered for three main reasons.

1   It was the largest uprising of the Tudor period and, as such, represented a clear rejection of Henry's key policies by a significant minority in his realm.

2   The Pilgrims were well-armed and led. If they had fought against the royal army, it is highly likely that they would have won.

3   The Pilgrims had forced the king into making concessions. Henry's first instinct was to crush the rebellion, but realising his weakness, he accepted the need for negotiations. He then granted a general pardon when initially he had wanted to punish ten leaders. Although short lived, the Pilgrims also secured the promise of a parliament and a halt to dissolution.

The Pilgrimage of Grace also brought about two further consequences. Monasteries were dissolved much quicker because Henry thought they were a potential focus for resistance. Also, the reformed Council of the North increased royal power in the North.

Interpretation 1

A leading Tudor historian, J.J Scarisbrick, outlined the significance of the rebellion in *Henry VIII*, 1997.

Moreover, the rebellion might well have been an even larger convulsion than it was. It could have openly enlisted latent Yorkist sentiment and thus acquired dynastic overtones; its fire might have spread to other parts of England; there could have been Scottish intervention; there were moves towards calling for help from the emperor. Finally, Rome was ready to intervene… The crown was scarcely in greater peril… and yet, presumably because it fought for the wrong side and because it failed, the Pilgrimage has often been treated by historians as a minor, peripheral upset wrought by a few provincial conservatives, a somewhat pathetic rising which could never have succeeded against Henry's solid regime. But the truth is that, if it had wanted, it might have swamped him.

Summary

- Henry VIII's religious changes were unpopular in the north of England. They helped spark an uprising known as the Pilgrimage of Grace. The first uprising, in Lincolnshire, failed.
- An uprising in Yorkshire developed under the leadership of Robert Aske.
- The main rebel demands focused on reversing Henry's religious reforms.
- Henry placed the Duke of Norfolk in charge of stopping the uprising.
- The uprising failed because the Pilgrims decided to trust Henry and negotiate with him, rather than fight.
- The king had no intention of keeping the promises he made to the Pilgrims, and in the spring of 1537 he rounded up and executed the rebel leaders.

Checkpoint

Strengthen

S1 List all the significant individuals involved in the Pilgrimage of Grace.

S2 What were the Pontefract Articles?

Challenge

C1 Outline the similarities and differences between the Lincolnshire and Yorkshire uprisings.

C2 Why was Henry VIII unable to crush the Pilgrimage of Grace by force?

How confident do you feel about your answers? Share your answers with a partner and see if you can improve them.

Recap: The Reformation and its impact, 1529–40

Recall questions

1 What was the sole religion of Western Europe, including England, at the start of Henry VIII's reign?

2 What was the name given to belief whereby bread and water was turned into the body and blood of Christ in the Mass?

3 Which religious leader started the Reformation in Europe?

4 Which high profile figure silently opposed Henry VIII becoming head of the English Church?

5 What significant event occurred in 1539 which many Protestant's approved of?

6 What law did Henry VIII pass in 1539 to put a stop to any further religious reforms in his Church?

7 What was the main role of monasteries?

8 What was the name of the survey carried out into the wealth of the monasteries?

9 Who led the Pilgrimage of Grace and which noble was sent to deal with him?

10 In order to end the Pilgrimage of Grace, what three things did Henry promise the rebels?

Exam-style question, Section B

Describe **two** features of John Fisher's opposition to Henry VIII. **4 marks**

Exam tip

Two relevant points would be Fisher's strong Catholic beliefs and his strategy of actively resisting Henry. Remember to bring in specific information to help explain these two features.

Activities

1 Go back and look at Figure 2.4 on page 49. It shows significant events in Henry's life in 1536. Using the information you have learned in Chapter 3, what significant events would you add to this timeline?

2 Once you have listed the events you would add, discuss with a partner which event was the most significant for Henry in 1536. Why do you think this?

3 Write a short paragraph explaining your answer.

Exam-style question, Section B

'The Pilgrimage of Grace was badly led'. Do you agree?

You may use the following in your answer:

- Robert Aske
- the agreement at Doncaster.

You **must** also use information of your own. **16 marks**

Exam tip

To do well in this question you need to provide an analytical answer. Include accurate and relevant historical knowledge, identify at least one point extra to those given in the question and reach an overall judgement.

Activities

1 Create a timeline for the years 1534–40, starting with the 1534 Act of Supremacy. Mark on all the key religious developments.

   a Now decide the degree to which each development was an advance for the Catholic or Protestant cause. Circle all Catholic developments on your timeline red, and Protestant developments blue.

   b Give each event a score out of ten; one representing a completely Catholic policy and ten a completely Protestant policy.

2 Overall, do you think the Catholics or the Protestants won the battle for the English Church in the years 1534–40?

WRITING HISTORICALLY

Writing historically: writing cohesively

When you explain events and their consequences, you need to make your explanation as clear and succinct as possible.

Learning outcomes

By the end of this lesson, you will understand how to:

- use pronouns to refer back to ideas earlier in your writing
- use sentence structures to help you refer back to ideas earlier in your writing clearly and economically.

Definition

Pronoun: a word that can stand in for, and refer back to, a noun, e.g. 'he', 'she', 'this', 'that', etc.

How can I refer back to earlier ideas as clearly as possible?

Look at the beginning of a response to this exam-style question below:

> 'Between 1534 and 1540 the English Church changed very little'. How far do you agree? **(16 marks)**

> *Before the Act of Supremacy, Rome ruled the Church, for example appointing leading clerics and collecting clerical taxes. This was a big change for the English Church.*

1. In the second sentence, the **pronoun** 'this' refers back to the first sentence. What could it refer back to?

   f. the Act of Supremacy

   g. Rome's rule

   h. appointing clerics and collecting taxes

   i. it's not clear – it could be referring to any or all of them

One way in which you can improve the clarity of your writing is to avoid imprecise pronouns like 'this' and either:

- repeat the idea you are referring back to OR
- replace it with a word or phrase that summarises the idea.

2. Which of these would you choose to replace 'this' with to make these sentences as clear and precise as possible?

   a. The Act of Supremacy

   b. The Act

   c. This 1534 Act

   d. The Act of 1534

> *Before the Act of Supremacy, Rome ruled the Church, for example appointing leading clerics and collecting clerical taxes. This was a big change for the English Church.*

3. Now look at some more sentences from the same response below. What could you replace 'This' with to make the sentences as clear as possible?

> Cromwell's next two Acts had a greater impact because the Ten Articles cut down the sacraments to three, the Injunctions attacked pilgrimages and limited Holy Days. This changed the daily experience of the Church enormously.

How can I structure my sentences to make referring back even clearer?

4. Look at the three versions below of sentences written in response to the exam-style question on the previous page:

Version A

> Before the introduction of the English Bible, most people were ignorant of Church services because they could not understand what was read to them. This was significant because people could read and interpret it themselves.

The pronoun 'this' is meant to refer back to this phrase – but, because it follows this clause, the writer has not made it clear what it refers to.

Version B

> Most people were ignorant of Church services because they could not understand what was read to them before the introduction of the English Bible. This was significant because people could read and interpret it themselves.

Version C

> Many people were ignorant of Church services before the introduction of the English Bible. This Royal Injunction was significant because people could read and interpret the Bible themselves.

Which version is most clearly expressed and therefore easiest to read? Write a sentence or two explaining your ideas, thinking about:

- the use of the pronoun 'this'
- the position of the idea it refers back to
- the use of word or phrase that summarises the idea.

Did you notice?

When you read a text, you usually assume that the pronoun 'this' refers back to the piece of information that you have just read – not the one before that, or the one, two, or three sentences ago.

5. Why are these sentences below unclear and difficult to make sense of?

> In 1538 icons and relics were removed from churches. People had worshipped these as well as saints before the Reformation. This proved the Protestant nature of the reforms.

Improving an answer

6. Experiment with two or three different ways of rearranging and / or rewriting the sentence fragments below to create sentences that explain as clearly as possible the impact of the English Bible.

> [1] There was a rush to read the Bible [2] when the English translation was first introduced [3] because people had not previously been able to read God's word. [4] This resulted in a wave of individual views and opinions.

Preparing for your GCSE Paper 2 exam

Paper 2 overview

Your Paper 2 is in two sections that examine the Period Study and British Depth Study. They each count for 20% of your History assessment. The questions on Henry VIII and his ministers, 1509–40, are the British Depth Study and are in Section B of the exam paper. You should save just over half the time allowed for Paper 2 to write your answers to Section B. This will give a few moments for checking your answers at the end.

History Paper 2	Period Study and British Depth Study			Time 1 hour 45 mins
Section A	Period Study	Answer 3 questions	32 marks	50 mins
Section B	Tudor Depth Option B3	Answer 3 questions	32 marks	55 mins

British Depth Option B3 Henry VIII and his ministers, 1509-40

You will answer Question 4, which is in three parts:

(a) Describe two features of...   (4 marks)

You are given a few lines to write about each feature. Allow five minutes to write your answer. It is only worth four marks, so keep the answer brief and try not to add more information on extra lines.

(b) Explain why...   (12 marks)

This question asks you to explain the reasons why something happened. Allow 20 minutes to write your answer. You are given two stimulus (information) points as prompts to help you. You do not have to use the prompts and you will not lose marks by leaving them out. Always remember to add in a new point of your own as well. Higher marks are gained by adding in a point extra to the prompts. You will be given at least two pages in the answer booklet for your answer. This does not mean you should try to fill all the space. The front page of the exam paper tells you 'there may be more space than you need'. Aim to give at least three explained reasons.

(c) (i) OR (ii) How far do you agree? (16 marks)

This question is worth half your marks for the whole of the Depth Study. Make sure you have kept 30 minutes to answer it. You have a choice of statements: (i) or (ii). Before you decide, be clear what the statement is about: what 'concept' it is about and what topic information you will need to respond to it. You will have prompts to help, as for part (b).

The statement can be about the concepts of: cause, significance, consequence, change, continuity, similarity or difference. It is a good idea during revision to practise identifying the concept focus of statements. You could do this with everyday examples and test one another: *the bus was late because it broke down = statement about cause; the bus broke down as a result of poor maintenance = statement about consequence; the bus service has improved recently = statement about change.*

You must make a judgement on **how far you agree** and you should think about **both** sides of the argument. Plan your answer before you begin to write and put your answer points in two columns: For and Against. You should consider at least three points. Think about it as if you were putting weight on each side to decide what your judgement is going to be for the conclusion. That way your whole answer hangs together – it is coherent. Be clear about your reasons (your criteria) for your judgement – for example: why one cause is more important than another? Did it perhaps set others in motion? You must **explain** your answer.

On the one hand	On the other hand
• Point 1	• Point 2
	• Point 3

Conclusion

Paper 2, Question 4a

Describe **two** features of the Field of the Cloth of Gold. **(4 marks)**

Average answer

The chief organiser of the Field of the Cloth of Gold was Cardinal Wolsey.

> A feature is identified but there is no development.

Its aim was to prevent war breaking out.

> Again a further valid feature is identified – the meeting's aim – but with no supporting information.

Verdict

This is an average answer because two valid features are given but with no supporting information.

Use the feedback to rewrite this answer, making as many improvements as you can.

Strong answer

The Field of the Cloth of Gold was a high level meeting arranged by Cardinal Wolsey between Henry VIII and Francis I, the King of France, in 1520. Both were young, ambitious rulers who were keen to impress each other.

> The answer has identified a feature – in this case who the leading participants were. Supporting information is directly related to it.

One of the aims of the meeting was to prevent war breaking out between Francis I and Charles V, the ruler of Spain and the Hapsburg Empire. Following the Treaty of London in 1518, Henry had taken on the role of European peacemaker.

> A further valid feature is identified – the meeting's aim – and the supporting information briefly develops this point.

Verdict

This is a strong answer because two valid features are given with supporting information.

Paper 2, Question 4b

Explain why Henry VIII decided to close down the monasteries.

You may use the following in your answer:

- monastery land
- Cromwell's commissions.

You **must** also use information of your own. **(12 marks)**

Exam tip

Focus on explaining 'why'. Aim to give at least three clear reasons to explain your answer.

Average answer

The monasteries were very wealthy, mainly due to the large amounts of land they owned and the fact that people often left them money in their wills. When the monasteries were closed, their treasures, including gold plate, were sent to London. Their land was sold off. Cromwell set up the Court of Augmentations to handle all this. Henry ordered the closure of the monasteries because he needed their money.

Cromwell discovered a lot of corruption because of his commissions. Two of his commissioners, Layton and Legh, visited 120 houses in 70 days. They questioned monks and nuns and many of them confessed to homosexual acts or having babies. Corruption was therefore a strong cause for the monasteries closure.

As a result of Henry's break with Rome, the pope had drawn up a papal bull. This said that England would be given to anyone who could take it. The monasteries were loyal to the pope first and to Henry second and this also explains why Henry closed them.

The information here is accurate but too descriptive. While there is good development about the wealth of monasteries, it is not linked to a full explanation of why this encouraged Henry to close down the monasteries. The end sentence begins to do this but is too brief.

While this information is valid, it does not explain why the stories of corruption in the monasteries mattered to Henry.

While this adds an important new point, it does not explain directly why Henry saw the monasteries' links with the pope as a danger and a reason for their closure.

Verdict

This is an average answer because:

- information is accurate, showing some knowledge and understanding of the period, and adds a point additional to the stimulus, so it is not a weak answer
- it does not analyse causes explicitly enough to be a strong answer
- there is some development of material, but the line of reasoning is not sustained.

Use the feedback to rewrite this answer, making as many improvements as you can.

Paper 2, Question 4b

Explain **why** Henry VIII decided to close down the monasteries. **(12 marks)**

....

Strong answer

At the start of Henry's reign, there were over 800 monasteries. By 1540, none were left. Henry ordered their closure for financial, moral and political reasons.

> An introduction is not strictly necessary, but the first sentence shows understanding of the question's context. Clear reasons are given in the second sentence to show the focus of the answer.

Money was the chief motivating factor for Henry. The monasteries were extremely wealthy institutions as they controlled nearly one-third of English land and had a total income of £160,000 a year, which was three times the money Henry received from his land. Henry discovered the extent of their wealth when Cromwell undertook a survey known as the 'Valor Eccelsiasticus'. The chance to gain this wealth was important because Henry needed money to fund his foreign policy aims. He wanted to achieve greatness through war. He also needed to strengthen England's defences. Ever since his split from Rome, Henry feared that Catholic Europe may invade and remove him.

> This paragraph begins with a valid point, provides specific information in support and ends with an explanation of its significance, tying the information to the question.

There were also concerns about the corruption of monks and nuns. In 1535, Cromwell's servants undertook a series of 'visitations' in order to assess the spiritual health of the monasteries. Visiting 120 houses in 70 days, many monks and nuns were questioned, often aggressively. This questioning resulted in many confessing to homosexual acts or having babies. Corruption was therefore a strong cause for the monasteries closure. Abuses like this were an important reason for closure because the monasteries were meant to be spiritually pure places, with monks and nuns married to God. This did not seem to be happening.

> This paragraph begins with a valid point. It is well-developed and effectively supported with some precise knowledge. Clear reasoning explains why this factor contributed to the closure of the monasteries.

Henry's concern about the loyalty of the monasteries was also significant. Henry wanted to be in total control of his kingdom. Many monasteries were loyal to Rome first, and Henry second. Also Henry feared that the security of his kingdom was in danger. As a result of Henry's break with Rome, the pope had drawn up a papal bull stating that England would be given to any Catholic ruler who could take it. The monasteries had strong links with Catholic countries in Europe that were a possible threat.

> A well chosen, additional reason beyond the stimulus points. The paragraph is also tied to the question, although it is slightly underdeveloped.

....

Verdict

This is a strong answer because:

- information is wide-ranging and is precisely selected to support points that directly address the question
- the explanation is analytical and directed consistently at the question
- the line of reasoning is coherent and sustained.

Paper 2, Question 4c

Anne Boleyn was executed because of the actions of Thomas Cromwell.

How far do you agree with this statement?

You may use the following in your answer:

- charges of adultery
- the birth of Elizabeth.

You **must** also use information of your own. **(16 marks)**

Exam tip

Consider points 'For' and 'Against' the statement and make a judgement. Be clear about your reasons for agreeing or disagreeing.

Average answer

Cromwell was Henry's chief minister and he was in charge of running the country for the king. He also played an important role in bringing about Anne Boleyn's execution. He was worried that she could bring about his own downfall, in the way that she had helped cause the fall of Wolsey in 1529. When Cromwell arrested Mark Smeaton, he found evidence that he was having an affair with the queen. Listening to court gossip, he then arrested four leading nobles included George Boleyn, Anne's own brother.

Anne Boleyn was also unlucky. She gave birth to a girl, Elizabeth, when Henry wanted a boy. She then had two miscarriages. Anne was then unlucky because Henry fell in love with Jane Seymour. He found Anne's personality too strong and he felt she was interfering too much in politics and religion. He thought Jane Seymour was sweet.

Anne was executed mainly because of the actions of Cromwell. He found evidence of adultery, which was enough to condemn her to death.

The first stimulus point is addressed and connected to the role of Cromwell. However, this paragraph is descriptive. Explaining why the information Cromwell gathered was so important to Anne Boleyn's execution would make the answer analytical.

Two points are given in this paragraph. The first concerns Henry's need for a boy, but it does not sufficiently explain why this point was so important. The second concerns the role of Jane Seymour. Although it also lacks development, it has attempted to provide a reason in addition to the two stimulus points.

A judgement is given, but overall the conclusion needs to be better explained. This can be done by briefly discussing the two other points developed in the answer and also explaining why they were of lesser importance.

Verdict

This is an average answer because:

- it shows some knowledge and understanding of the period, and adds a point additional to the stimulus, so is not a weak answer
- it mainly describes the points instead of explaining why they were important in bringing about Anne's downfall and so cannot be a strong answer
- it does not explain criteria for judgement clearly enough to be a strong answer.

Use the feedback to rewrite this answer, making as many improvements as you can.

Paper 2, Question 4c

Anne Boleyn was executed because of the actions of Thomas Cromwell. How far do you agree with this statement? **(16 marks)**

Strong answer

Cromwell played an important role in bringing about the execution of Anne Boleyn, but Henry's need for a son was the main factor.

After being ordered to investigate the private life of Anne Boleyn by Henry VIII, Cromwell found evidence of adultery with five men, including Mark Smeaton, and members of the high nobility. This information was important: the evidence Cromwell collected was presented at Anne's trial in May 1536 and proved enough to convict her of treason.

The most important reason for Anne Boleyn's execution was Henry's need for a son. By 1536, Anne had given birth to a daughter, Elizabeth, and miscarried on two occasions. This has to be seen as the most important reason because Henry needed a son in order to ensure the Tudor royal line remained strong after his death. He believed that England would be politically unstable under a female ruler and civil war could result. Furthermore, Henry's search for a son had already led him to divorce Catherine of Aragon. Finally, Henry was growing old. He was 45 in 1536 and injured from a jousting accident. The need to secure the succession was the most important thing on his mind.

Although not as important, Anne Boleyn was also executed because Henry had fallen in love with Jane Seymour... [Answer exemplifies the reasons why this was a factor.]

I only partly agree with the view that Anne Boleyn was executed because of the actions of Thomas Cromwell. He did play an important role by building a case of adultery against Anne Boleyn. However, he was merely carrying out the king's wishes. Ultimately, Henry decided that Anne Boleyn had to go because she could not provide him with a son. It is likely that had Anne Boleyn provided him with a son, her position would have been secure.

The context in the first sentence is brief but relevant. It directly addresses the question and sets out the overall line of argument.

This paragraph addresses the first bullet point and connects it to the role of Cromwell. The writing also explains why the charges of adultery mattered.

This paragraph is a good example of analytical writing because it explains why Henry's need for a son was so important.

A strong conclusion. A clear judgement on the question is made in the first sentence. All three points are then discussed. The importance of each point is also explained.

Verdict

This is a strong answer because:

- information is wide-ranging and is precisely selected to support points that directly address the question
- factors are analysed, exemplified and evaluated
- the line of reasoning is coherent and sustained, and the judgement is appropriately justified.

Answers to Henry Recap Questions

Chapter 1

1 2.5 million
2 Catherine of Aragon had initially been married to Henry VIII's brother, Arthur, although she claimed that the marriage had never been consummated
3 The Royal Household, Privy Chamber, Royal Council, Court, Parliament and Justices of the Peace
4 Lord Chancellor
5 £322,000
6 A list of rules drawn up by Wolsey in 1526 to make the running of Henry's palaces more cost effective
7 Francis I, King of France and Charles V, Emperor of the Holy Roman Empire and King of Spain
8 Following Charles V victory at Pavia, Wolsey abandoned England's traditional hostility to France and sided with Francis I against the Habsburg Emperor; the Treaty of More was signed in 1525
9 His failure to have a son with Catherine and the passage from Leviticus which seemed to prohibit marriage to a brother's widow
10 The Boleyn faction

Chapter 2

1 1523
2 Anne Boleyn had committed adultery
3 Jane Seymour
4 Jane Seymour gave birth to a son, the future Edward VI
5 Court of Augmentations and the Court of First Fruits and Tenths
6 The King's Chamber in the Royal Household
7 333 Acts
8 Thomas Howard, the 3rd Duke of Norfolk
9 Cromwell was made Earl of Essex
10 Henry married Catherine Howard

Chapter 3

1 Roman Catholicism
2 Transubstantiation
3 Martin Luther
4 Thomas More
5 The publication of the Great Bible
6 The Six Articles
7 To pray for the souls of the dead in order to ease their way through purgatory
8 The Valor Ecclesiasticus
9 Robert Aske led the Pilgrimage of Grace and Thomas Howard, the Duke of Norfolk, was sent to deal with him
10 A full pardon, a call of parliament and no further monastery closures until the parliament met

Index

Key terms are capitalised initially, in bold type with an asterisk.
Entry headings for topic booklets are shown in italics.

Acknowledgements

Picture Credits

The publisher would like to thank the following for their kind permission to reproduce their photographs:

(Key: b-bottom; c-centre; l-left; r-right; t-top)

Alamy Images: ACTIVE MUSEUM 6tl, 10, GL Archive 36, 39, 56, Heritage Image Partnership Ltd 60, Ian Dagnall 79, Ivy Close Images 44, Lebrecht Music and Arts Photo Library 15, 66, 78, Lordprice Collection 29, PAINTING 8, 24, 75, Tom Taylor 6bl, World History Archive 47; **Bridgeman Art Library Ltd:** His Grace The Duke of Norfolk, Arundel Castle 86, Private Collection / Photo © Philip Mould Ltd, London 58; **Getty Images:** The Print Collector 9

Cover images: *Front:* **Bridgeman Art Library Ltd:** Palazzo Barberini, Rome, Italy

All other images © Pearson Education

Text

We are grateful to the following for permission to reproduce copyright material:

Extract in Interpretation 1 on page 16 from *Henry VIII* Yale University Press (Scarisbrick, JJ 1997) pp.45-46; Extract in Interpretation 1 on page 31 from *Henry VIII*, Routledge (Wooding, L 2009) p.150, with permission from Routledge; Extract on page 37 from *Thomas Cromwell The untold story*, Hodder (Borman, T 2015) p.13, Hodder and Stoughton with permission; Extract on page 37 from *Thomas Cromwell The untold story*, Hodder (Borman,T 2015) p.21, Hodder and Stoughton with permission; Extract in Interpretation 1 on page 46 from *Thomas Cromwell The untold story*, Hodder (Borman, T 2015) pp.232, 236, Hodder and Stoughton with permission; Extract on page 75 from *Sir Thomas More and the Heretic*, History Today, Feb 1980 Vol 30 Issue 2 (J.A.Guy), with permission; Extract in Interpretation 1 on page 76 from *Sir Thomas More: saint or sinner?*, Telegraph, 20/01/2015 (Stanford, P), Telegraph Media Group Ltd 2015; Extract in Source C on page 84 from *Henry VIII*, Routledge (Wooding, L 2009) p. 213, with permission from Routledge; Extract on page 90 from *Henry VIII*, Yale (Scarisbrick, JJ 1997) pp. 341-342.